It Is Better to

Look Up

It Is Better to *Look Up*

LIFE EXPERIENCES SHARED FROM THE PULPIT

DESERET
BOOK

SALT LAKE CITY, UTAH

Royalties from this book
will benefit the general missionary fund
of The Church of Jesus Christ
of Latter-day Saints.

Library of Congress Cataloging-in-Publication Data

It is better to look up : life experiences shared from the pulpit.
    pages cm
  Includes index.
  Summary: A collection of more than fifty inspiring stories shared over the years by General Authorities of The Church of Jesus Christ of Latter-day Saints.
  ISBN 978-1-60907-947-5 (hardbound : alk. paper)
  1. Mormons—Conduct of life—Anecdotes. 2. The Church of Jesus Christ of Latter-day Saints—Doctrines.
  BX8656.I8 2014
  248.4'89332—dc23   2014019681

Printed in Canada
Friesens Corporation, Manitoba, Canada

10   9   8   7   6   5   4   3   2   1

CONTENTS

LIFT UP YOUR HEADS
and receive the pleasing word of God,
and feast upon his love; for ye may,
if your minds are firm, forever.

—Jacob 3:2

What Can
I Give?

ELDER NEIL L. ANDERSEN

*Therefore, O ye that embark in the
service of God, see that ye serve him
with all your heart, might, mind and
strength, that ye may stand blameless
before God at the last day.*
—*D&C 4:2*

*M*issionary service requires sacrifice. There will always be something you leave behind when you respond to the prophet's call to serve.

Those who follow the game of rugby know that the New Zealand All Blacks, a name given because of the color of their uniform, is the most celebrated rugby team ever. To be selected for the All Blacks in New Zealand would be comparable to playing for a football Super Bowl team or a World Cup soccer team.

In 1961, at age 18 and holding the Aaronic Priesthood, Sidney Going was becoming a star in

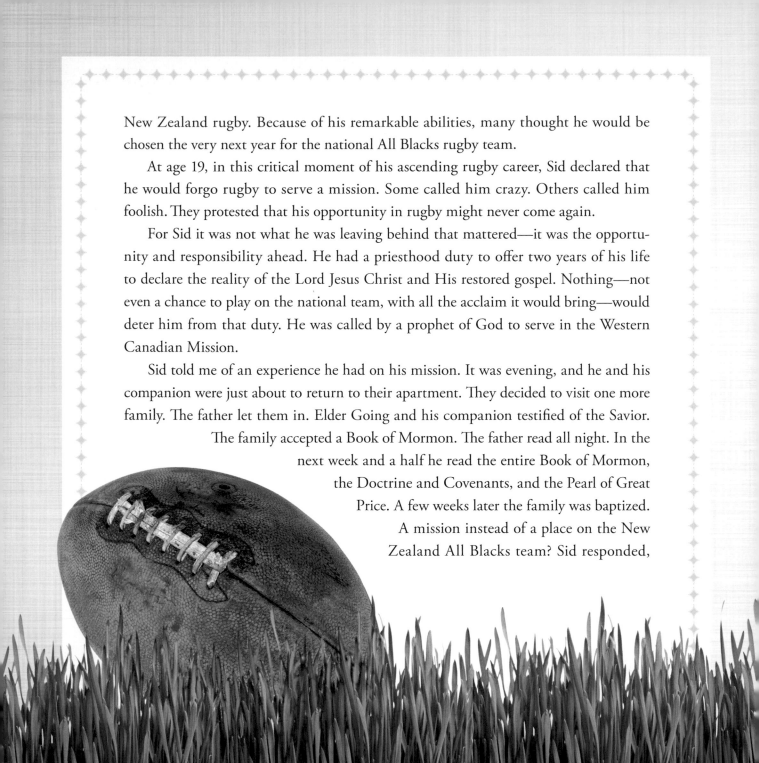

New Zealand rugby. Because of his remarkable abilities, many thought he would be chosen the very next year for the national All Blacks rugby team.

At age 19, in this critical moment of his ascending rugby career, Sid declared that he would forgo rugby to serve a mission. Some called him crazy. Others called him foolish. They protested that his opportunity in rugby might never come again.

For Sid it was not what he was leaving behind that mattered—it was the opportunity and responsibility ahead. He had a priesthood duty to offer two years of his life to declare the reality of the Lord Jesus Christ and His restored gospel. Nothing—not even a chance to play on the national team, with all the acclaim it would bring—would deter him from that duty. He was called by a prophet of God to serve in the Western Canadian Mission.

Sid told me of an experience he had on his mission. It was evening, and he and his companion were just about to return to their apartment. They decided to visit one more family. The father let them in. Elder Going and his companion testified of the Savior.

The family accepted a Book of Mormon. The father read all night. In the next week and a half he read the entire Book of Mormon, the Doctrine and Covenants, and the Pearl of Great Price. A few weeks later the family was baptized.

A mission instead of a place on the New Zealand All Blacks team? Sid responded,

"The blessing of [bringing others] into the gospel far outweighs anything [you] will ever sacrifice."

You're probably wondering what happened to Sid Going following his mission. Most important: an eternal marriage to his sweetheart, Colleen; five noble children; and a generation of grandchildren. He has lived his life trusting in his Father in Heaven, keeping the commandments, and serving others.

And rugby? After his mission Sid Going became one of the greatest halfbacks in All Blacks history, playing for 11 seasons and serving for many years as captain of the team.

How good was Sid Going? He was so good that training and game schedules were changed because he would not play on Sunday. Sid was so good the Queen of England acknowledged his contribution to rugby. He was so good a book was written about him titled *Super Sid*.

What if those honors had not come to Sid after his mission? One of the great miracles of missionary service in this Church is that Sid Going and thousands just like him have not asked, "What will I get from my mission?" but rather, "What can I give?"

Your mission will be a sacred opportunity to bring others to Christ and help prepare for the Second Coming of the Savior.

"You Stupid Cow!"

ELDER MERVYN B. ARNOLD

Do not suppose, because it has been spoken concerning restoration, that ye shall be restored from sin to happiness. Behold, I say unto you, wickedness never was happiness.

—Alma 41:10

Shortly after my sweetheart, Devonna, and I were married, she shared with me a story about how she learned in her youth the important doctrine that we are free to choose but that we are not free to choose the consequences of our actions:

"When I was 15 years old, I often felt that there were too many rules and commandments. I wasn't sure that a normal, fun-loving teenager could enjoy life with so many restrictions. Furthermore, the many hours spent working on my father's ranch were seriously dipping into my time with my friends.

"This particular summer, one of my jobs was to ensure that the cows grazing on the mountain pasture did not break through the fence and get into the wheat field. A cow grazing on the growing wheat can bloat, causing suffocation and death. One cow in particular was always trying to stick her head through the fence. One morning, as I was riding my horse along the fence line checking on the cattle, I found that the cow had broken through the fence and gotten into the wheat field. To my dismay, I realized that she had been eating wheat for quite some time because she was already bloated and looked much like a balloon. I thought, 'You stupid cow! That fence was there to protect you, yet you broke through it and you have eaten so much wheat that your life is in danger.'

"I raced back to the farmhouse to get my dad. However, when we returned, I found her lying dead on the ground. I was saddened by the loss of that cow. We had provided her with a beautiful mountain pasture to graze in and a fence to keep her away from the dangerous wheat, yet she foolishly broke through the fence and caused her own death.

"As I thought about the role of the fence, I realized that it was a protection, just as the commandments and my parents' rules were a protection. The commandments and rules were for my own good. I realized that obedience to the commandments could save me from physical and spiritual death. That enlightenment was a pivotal point in my life."

Sister Arnold learned that our kind, wise, and loving Heavenly Father has given us commandments not to restrict us, as the adversary would have us believe, but to bless our lives and to protect our good name and our legacy for future generations. Just like the cow that received the consequences of her choice, each one of us must learn that the grass is *never* greener on the other side of the fence—nor will it ever be, for "wickedness never was happiness." Each one of us will receive the consequences of our choices when this life is over. The commandments are clear, they are protective—they are not restrictive—and the wonderful blessings of obedience are numberless! 🐾

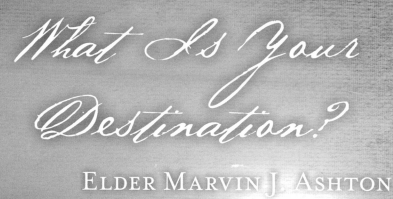

What Is Your Destination?

ELDER MARVIN J. ASHTON

*Jesus saith unto him, I am the way, the truth, and
the life: no man cometh unto the Father, but by me.*
—John 14:6

While on an assignment in England, I had the opportunity to do some traveling by train. Weather and time schedules indicated this to be the most satisfactory method of transportation.

One day as the train rolled from Manchester to Leicester, after about an hour and a half of reading, I put down my books, looked out the window, and wondered if we were getting close to the station. A few minutes later the door to the compartment opened and the conductor entered. He greeted me with, "What is your destination?"

Inasmuch as I had been giving some thought to arrivals, departures, and stops, I answered, "I have an appointment in Leicester."

To this he responded with, "We shall be at your destination in ten minutes." He punched my ticket and made his way to check others.

After he left, I pondered his comments, "What is your destination?" and "We shall be at your destination in ten minutes." He seemed convinced that every time the train stopped and dozens or hundreds of people got off, they had arrived at their destinations. Apparently he had been announcing this to his passengers for years.

However, I knew, despite his comments, that I needed to be in Leicester for two days for quarterly stake conference sessions but that it was not my destination. Stops in other English cities were not my destinations either. They were all assignments along the way. I had not arrived when I reached any of them.

As a result of this experience on the train, and having given this thought some consideration over the years, I am concerned that many of us are confused in our life's travels with destinations, arrivals, stops, calls, stations, and assignments. It appears to me that some of us may be lost today because we think we have arrived. . . .

Have you reached your destination when you receive a testimony of the truthfulness of the gospel of Jesus Christ by revelation from the Holy Ghost? We are sorry to observe that some, having received a testimony, feel and respond as if they had arrived. What a sad day in the life of any individual when he fails to use this knowledge and conviction of a testimony for dedicated and continued service. A testimony grows as it is shared. With the possession of a testimony comes the obligation to bear witness to the world of this, the Lord's work. A testimony is not a destination; it is a possession for performance.

Have you reached your destination when you are baptized, become an elder, a bishop, a stake president, a Relief Society officer, a seventy, or an apostle? In these days of needed performance and service it is hoped all of us will emphatically respond to this question with a resounding NO! . . .

As we pursue our journeys, let us ever bear in mind that in train travel and in life, there are stations, there are departures, calls, schedules, and opportunities for being sidetracked and diverted. Wise is the individual who follows in His, the Savior's, paths. Safety and joy belong to those who will come and follow Him. I bear witness that God is eternal. We are eternal, and God never intended for us to travel alone.

Precious Flecks of Gold

ELDER M. RUSSELL BALLARD

By small and simple things are great things brought to pass; and small means in many instances doth confound the wise. And the Lord God doth work by means to bring about his great and eternal purposes.
—Alma 37:6–7

A young merchant from Boston was caught up in the fervor of the 1849 California gold rush. He sold all of his possessions to seek his fortune in the California rivers, which he was told were filled with gold nuggets so big that one could hardly carry them.

Day after endless day, the young man dipped his pan into the river and came up empty. His only reward was a growing pile of rocks. Discouraged and broke, he was ready to quit until one day an old, experienced prospector said to him, "That's quite a pile of rocks you are getting there, my boy."

The young man replied, "There's no gold here. I'm going back home."

Walking over to the pile of rocks, the old prospector said, "Oh, there is gold all right. You just have to know where to find it." He picked two rocks up in his hands and crashed them together. One of the rocks split open, revealing several flecks of gold sparkling in the sunlight.

Noticing a bulging leather pouch fastened to the prospector's waist, the young man said, "I'm looking for nuggets like the ones in your pouch, not just tiny flecks."

The old prospector extended his pouch toward the young man, who looked inside, expecting to see several large nuggets. He was stunned to see that the pouch was filled with thousands of flecks of gold.

The old prospector said, "Son, it seems to me you are so busy looking for large nuggets that you're missing filling your pouch with these precious flecks of gold. The patient accumulation of these little flecks has brought me great wealth."

This story illustrates the spiritual truth that Alma taught his son Helaman:

"By small and simple things are great things brought to pass. . . . And by very small means the Lord . . . bringeth about the salvation of many souls" (Alma 37:6–7).

The gospel of Jesus Christ is simple, no matter how much we try to make it complicated. We should strive to keep our lives similarly simple, unencumbered by extraneous influences, focused on those things that matter most.

ELDER MERRILL J. BATEMAN

The Spirit of the Lord is upon me, because he hath anointed me to preach the gospel to the poor; he hath sent me to heal the brokenhearted, to preach deliverance to the captives, and recovering of sight to the blind.
—Luke 4:18

Sister Bateman and I were touring the Japan Fukuoka Mission when the missionaries in Kumamoto introduced us to a young Japanese brother who had just joined the Church and then told us of his conversion. He was from a non-Christian background. When he met the missionaries, he was interested in the message. He liked the young men who were teaching him, but during the course of the lessons he could not understand or feel the need for a Savior. The missionaries took him through the lessons and taught him about our Heavenly Father, Christ, and the plan of salvation, but he didn't have a witness. The missionaries wondered what they should do and decided one day to show him a film, a Church film that deals with the Atonement. It is called *The Bridge.* The young man saw the film and was disturbed by it, went home, and couldn't sleep all that night, but still he didn't have a witness.

The next morning he went to work. He worked in an optician's shop making eyeglasses. During the course of the day, an elderly woman came in. He remembered her coming in a few weeks before. She had broken her glasses. She needed a new pair. When she had come in earlier, she didn't have enough money and had gone away to save more in order to purchase the new glasses. As she came in that day, she again showed him her spectacles and showed him the money that she now had. He realized that she didn't have enough yet. Then a thought came to him: *I have some money. I don't need to tell her. I can make up the difference.* So he told her the money she had was adequate, took her glasses, made an appointment for her to return when he had finished making the spectacles, and sent her on her way.

She returned later. He had the glasses ready for her. He handed them to her, and she put them on. *"Miemasu! Miemasu!* I see. I see." Then she began to cry. At that point, a burning sensation began to grow within his bosom and swelled within him. He said, *"Wakari masu! Wakari masu!* I understand. I understand." He began to cry. Out the door he ran, looking for the missionaries. When he found them, he said, "I see! My eyes have been opened! I know that Jesus is the Son of God. I know the stone was rolled away from the tomb and on that glorious Easter morning He arose from the dead. He can make up the difference in my life when I fall short."

ヨ

谷 生

竜 羊 王

亀 王 允 尢

自 夂 疋 舌 冊

A Heavy Load

ELDER DAVID A. BEDNAR

*The Lord did strengthen them that they could bear up
their burdens with ease, and they did submit cheerfully
and with patience to all the will of the Lord.*
—Mosiah 24:15

I have a dear friend who, in the early years of his marriage, was convinced he and his family needed a four-wheel-drive pickup truck. His wife was sure that he did not need but merely wanted the new vehicle. A playful conversation between this husband and wife initiated their consideration of the advantages and dis-advantages of such a purchase.

"Sweetheart, we need a four-wheel-drive truck."

She asked, "Why do you think we need a new truck?"

He answered her question with what he believed was the perfect response: "What if we needed milk for our children in a terrible storm, and the only way I could get to the grocery store was in a pickup?"

His wife replied with a smile, "If we buy a new truck, we will not have money for milk—so why worry about getting to the store in an emergency!"

Over time they continued to counsel together and ultimately decided to acquire the truck. Shortly after taking possession of the new vehicle, my friend wanted to demonstrate the utility of the truck and validate his reasons for wanting to purchase it. So he decided he would cut and haul a supply of firewood for their home. It was in the autumn of the year, and snow already had fallen in the mountains where he intended to find wood. As he drove up the mountainside, the snow gradually became deeper and deeper. My friend recognized the slick road conditions presented a risk, but with great confidence in the new truck, he kept going.

Sadly, my friend went too far along the snowy road. As he steered the truck off of the road at the place he had determined to cut wood, he got stuck. All four of the wheels on the new truck spun in the snow. He readily recognized that he did

not know what to do to extricate himself from this dangerous situation. He was embarrassed and worried.

My friend decided, "Well, I will not just sit here." He climbed out of the vehicle and started cutting wood. He completely filled the back of the truck with the heavy load. And then my friend determined he would try driving out of the snow one more time. As he put the pickup into gear and applied power, he started to inch forward. Slowly the truck moved out of the snow and back onto the road. He finally was free to go home, a happy and humbled man. . . .

It was the load of wood that provided the traction necessary for him to get out of the snow, to get back on the road, and to move forward. It was the load that enabled him to return to his family and his home.

Each of us also carries a load. Our individual load is comprised of demands and opportunities, obligations and privileges, afflictions and blessings, and options and constraints. Two guiding questions can be helpful as we periodically and prayerfully assess our load: "Is the load I am carrying producing the spiritual traction that will enable me to press forward with faith in Christ on the strait and narrow path and avoid getting stuck? Is the load I am carrying creating sufficient spiritual traction so I ultimately can return home to Heavenly Father?"

Sometimes we mistakenly may believe that happiness is the absence of a load. But bearing a load is a necessary and essential part of the plan of happiness. Because our individual load needs to generate spiritual traction, we should be careful to not haul around in our lives so many nice but unnecessary things that we are distracted and diverted from the things that truly matter most. 🪶

A Lesson in Obedience

PRESIDENT EZRA TAFT BENSON

Blessed are ye, when men shall revile you, and persecute you,
and shall say all manner of evil against you falsely, for my sake. Rejoice,
and be exceeding glad: for great is your reward in heaven.
—Matthew 5:11–12

In 1923 I was serving a mission in Great Britain. At that time there was great opposition to the Church. It began with the ministers and then spread through the press. Many anti-Mormon articles appeared in the daily press. A number of anti-Mormon movies were shown, and derogatory plays were produced on the stage. The general theme was the same—that Mormon missionaries were in England to lure away British girls and make slaves of them on Utah farms. Today that seems fantastic, but in those days it was very real. In some places we even had to stop tracting because of such misunderstandings.

One time we received a letter from mission headquarters instructing us that we should discontinue all street meetings. At that time I was serving as the conference president, and my companion was the conference clerk. When this instruction arrived, we already had a meeting scheduled for the following Sunday night. So we reasoned that we would hold that meeting and then discontinue street meetings thereafter. That's where we made our mistake!

The next Sunday evening we held our street meeting down near the railway station as scheduled. The crowd was large and unruly. In our efforts to preach to them, my

companion and I stood back to back. He spoke in one direction, and I faced the other half of the crowd.

When the saloons closed, the rougher, coarser element came out on the streets, many under the influence of liquor. The crowd became noisy, and those on the outside were not able to hear too well.

Some yelled, "What's the excitement?"

Others yelled back, "It's those dreadful Mormons."

To this, others responded, "Let's get them and throw them in the river."

Soon an attempt was made to trample us under their feet. But since we were taller than the average man there, we put our hands on their shoulders and prevented them from getting us under their feet.

During the excitement, my companion and I became separated. They took him down the far side of the railway station and me down the near side. Things began to look pretty bad.

Then a big, husky fellow came up to me as some of the others formed a circle around me about ten feet in diameter. The man looked me straight in the eye and said, "Young man, I believe every word you said tonight!"

By this time a British policeman had worked his way through the crowd. He took me by the arm and said,

"Young man, you come with me. You're lucky to be alive in this crowd." He led me several blocks and then ordered, "Now you get to your lodge and don't come out anymore tonight."

When I arrived at the lodge, I found that my companion was not yet there. I worried and then prayed and waited. I became so concerned about him that I decided to disguise my appearance by putting on an old American cap and taking off my topcoat. Then I went out to try to find him.

As I neared the place of the meeting, a man recognized me and asked, "Have you seen your companion?"

I said, "No. Where is he?"

He responded, "He's down on the other side of the railway station with one side of his head mashed in."

This frightened me greatly, and I sprinted to the site as fast as I could. Before I reached the railway station, however, I met the same policeman again. He said, "I thought I told you to stay in and not come out on the street again tonight."

I replied, "You did, officer. But I'm concerned about my companion. Do you know where he is?"

He replied, "Yes, he got a nasty blow on the side of his head, but he's gone to the lodge now. I walked partway with him as I did earlier with you. Now you get back there and don't come out anymore tonight."

So I went back to the lodge and found my companion disguising himself in order to go out and look for me. We threw our arms around each other and knelt together in prayer. From that experience I learned always to follow counsel, and that lesson has followed me all the days of my life. 🪶

The Savior Is
Counting on You

ELDER JOE J. CHRISTENSEN

By this shall all men know that ye are my disciples,
if ye have love one to another.
—John 13:35

The Savior is counting on you to be a champion of those who need you, and they are all around you—in your school, in your neighborhood, in your family.

At a 20-year high school reunion, one of the graduates had a surprising conversation with one of her classmates that went something like this:

"I came to this reunion after all these years hoping you would be here so I could thank you. My high school experience was hard for me. You may not have known it, but you were the only friend I had in high school. I wondered if maybe the seminary teacher had assigned you to be nice to me. Did he?"

"No. He didn't assign me."

"Well, you didn't know it, but every day I looked for you because I knew that you would talk to me. You made me feel better about myself. Now I am married and have a large family. During these past years I have thought many times of what you meant to me, and I wanted to tell you that."

There are those who wake up every morning dreading to go to school, or even to a Church activity, because they worry about how they will be treated. You have the power to change their lives for the better.

Elder D. Todd Christofferson

I will go before your face. I will be on
your right hand and on your left, and my
Spirit shall be in your hearts, and mine
angels round about you, to bear you up.
—D&C 84:88

In 1992 two sister missionaries in Zagreb, Croatia, were returning to their apartment one evening. Their last teaching appointment had been some distance away, and it was getting dark. Several men on the trolley made crude comments and became rather menacing. Feeling threatened, the sisters got off the trolley at the next stop just as the doors closed so no one could follow them. Having avoided that problem, they realized they were in a place unknown to either of them. As they turned to look for help, they saw a woman. The missionaries explained that they were lost and asked the woman if she could direct them. She knew where they could find another

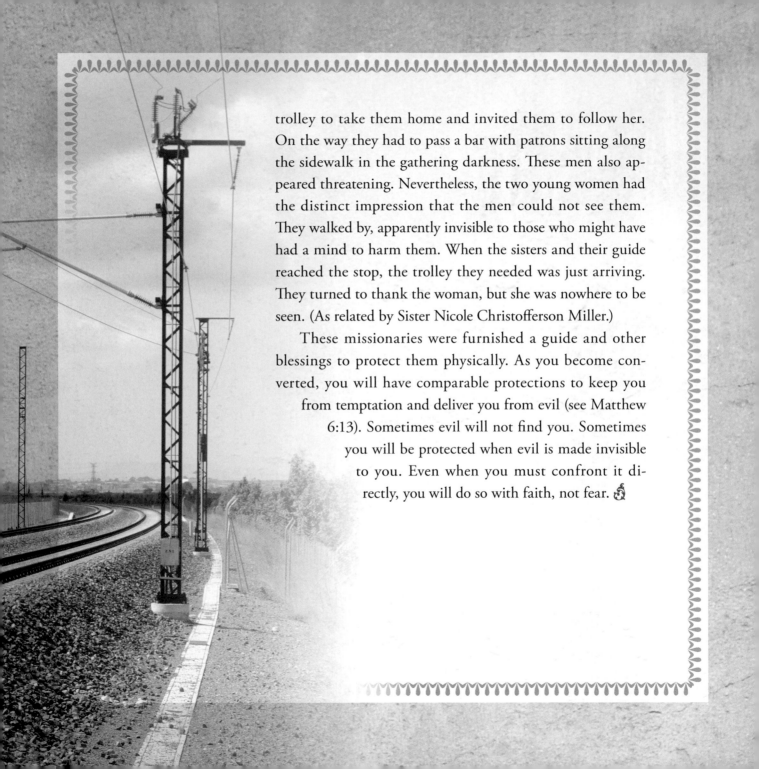

trolley to take them home and invited them to follow her. On the way they had to pass a bar with patrons sitting along the sidewalk in the gathering darkness. These men also appeared threatening. Nevertheless, the two young women had the distinct impression that the men could not see them. They walked by, apparently invisible to those who might have had a mind to harm them. When the sisters and their guide reached the stop, the trolley they needed was just arriving. They turned to thank the woman, but she was nowhere to be seen. (As related by Sister Nicole Christofferson Miller.)

These missionaries were furnished a guide and other blessings to protect them physically. As you become converted, you will have comparable protections to keep you from temptation and deliver you from evil (see Matthew 6:13). Sometimes evil will not find you. Sometimes you will be protected when evil is made invisible to you. Even when you must confront it directly, you will do so with faith, not fear.

It Is Better to Look Up

ELDER CARL B. COOK

Look up, and lift up your heads; for your redemption draweth nigh.
—Luke 21:28

At the end of a particularly tiring day toward the end of my first week as a General Authority, my briefcase was overloaded and my mind was preoccupied with the question, "How can I possibly do this?" I left the office of the Seventy and entered the elevator of the Church Administration Building. As the elevator descended, my head was down and I stared blankly at the floor.

The door opened and someone entered, but I didn't look up. As the door closed, I heard someone ask, "What are you looking at down there?" I recognized that voice—it was President Thomas S. Monson.

I quickly looked up and responded, "Oh, nothing." (I'm sure that clever response inspired confidence in my abilities!)

But he had seen my subdued countenance and my heavy briefcase. He smiled and lovingly suggested, while pointing heavenward, "It is better to look up!" As we traveled down one more level, he cheerfully explained that he was on his way to the temple. When he bid me farewell, his parting glance spoke again to my heart, "Now, remember, it is better to look up."

As we parted, the words of a scripture came to mind: "Believe in God; believe that he is . . . ; believe that he has all wisdom, and all power, both in heaven and in earth" (Mosiah 4:9). As I thought of Heavenly Father and Jesus Christ's power, my heart found the comfort I had sought in vain from the floor of that descending elevator.

Since then I have pondered this experience and the role of prophets. I was burdened and my head was down. As the prophet spoke, I looked to him. He redirected my focus to look up to God, where I could be healed and strengthened through Christ's Atonement. That is what prophets do for us. They lead us to God. 🔥

There Is Nothing the Love of Christ Cannot Heal

ELDER
QUENTIN L. COOK

Wherefore, be of good cheer, and
do not fear, for I the Lord am with
you, and will stand by you.
—D&C 68:6

*L*et me share with you the true account of one sister, Ellen Yates from Grantsville, Utah. One October day she kissed her husband, Leon, good-bye as he left to go to work in Salt Lake City. This would be the last time she would see Leon alive. He was involved in an accident with a young man 20 years of age who was late for his first job and had tried to pass a slower vehicle, resulting in a head-on collision that killed them both instantly. Sister Yates said that after two compassionate highway patrolmen told her the news, she plunged into shock and grief.

She records, "As I tried to look ahead in life, all I could see was darkness and pain." It turned out that her husband's best friend was the bishop of the young man's ward. The bishop called Sister Yates and told her that the young man's mother, Jolayne Willmore, wanted to talk with her. She remembers "being shocked because I was so centered on my grief and pain that I had not even thought about the young man and his family. I suddenly realized that here was a mother who was in as much or more pain than I was. I quickly gave my permission . . . for a visit."

When Brother and Sister Willmore arrived, they expressed their great sorrow that their son was responsible for Leon's death and presented Sister Yates with a picture of the Savior holding a little girl in His arms. Sister Yates says, "When times become too hard to bear, I look at this picture and remember that Christ knows me personally. He knows my loneliness and my trials." One scripture that comforts Sister Yates is "Wherefore, be of good cheer, and do not fear, for I the Lord am with you, and will stand by you" (D&C 68:6).

Each October Sister Yates and Sister Willmore go to the temple together and offer thanks for the Atonement of Jesus Christ, for the plan of salvation, for eternal families, and for the covenants that bind together husbands and wives and families on both sides of the veil. Sister Yates concludes, "Through this trial, I have felt the love of my Father in Heaven and my Savior in greater abundance than I had ever felt before." She testifies that "there is no grief, no pain, no sickness so great that the Atonement of Christ and the love of Christ cannot heal." What a wonderful example of love and forgiveness these two sisters have demonstrated. It has allowed the Atonement of Jesus Christ to be efficacious in their lives. 🐚

"Act Well
Thy Part"

SISTER ELAINE S. DALTON

Stand as witnesses of God at all times and in all things, and in all places.
—Mosiah 18:9

When I was in college, I was a member of the BYU International Folk Dancers. One summer our group had the unique privilege to tour the missions in Europe. It was a difficult summer for me because a few months earlier my father had unexpectedly passed away. While we were in Scotland, I felt especially alone and became discouraged. We danced at a chapel that night, and then after our performance we went next door to the mission home. As I proceeded up the walk, I saw a stone placed in a well-kept garden by the gate. On it I read the words, "What-e'er thou art, act well thy part." At that moment those words went deeply into my heart, and I felt the powers of heaven reach out and give me a message. I knew I was known by a loving Heavenly Father. I felt I was not alone. I stood in that garden with tears in my eyes. "What-e'er thou art, act well thy part." That simple statement renewed my vision that Heavenly Father knew me and had a plan for my life, and the spirit I felt helped me understand that my part mattered.

Later I learned that this saying had once motivated the prophet David O. McKay while he was serving as a young missionary in Scotland. He had seen it on a stone on a building at a discouraging time in his life and on his mission, and the words lifted him. Years later, as the building was being torn down, he made arrangements to obtain the stone and had it placed in the garden at the mission home. . . .

Several years ago, as the Conference Center in Salt Lake City was being built and nearing completion, I entered that sacred building on the balcony level in a hard hat and safety glasses, ready to vacuum the carpet that my husband was helping to install. Where the rostrum now stands was a front-end loader moving dirt, and the dust in the building was thick. When it settled, it did so on the new carpet. My part was to vacuum. And so I vacuumed and vacuumed and vacuumed. After three days my little vacuum burned up!

The afternoon before the first general conference in that beautiful building, my husband called me. He was about to install the last piece of carpet—under the historic pulpit. He asked, "What scripture should I write on the back of this carpet?"

And I said, "Mosiah 18:9: 'Stand as [a witness] of God at all times and in all things, and in all places.'"

In an extremely challenging world, that is what I see young women and women of this Church doing. They are an influence for good. They are virtuous and exemplary, intelligent and industrious. They are making a difference because they are different. They are acting well their part.

Years ago when I was vacuuming so diligently—trying to act well my small part—I didn't realize that I would one day stand with my feet on that very piece of carpet. 🔖

Saving
Souls

BISHOP RICHARD C. EDGLEY

O Lord, wilt thou grant unto us that we may have success in bringing them again unto thee in Christ. Behold, O Lord, their souls are precious, and many of them are our brethren; therefore, give unto us, O Lord, power and wisdom that we may bring these, our brethren, again unto thee.

—Alma 31:34–35

One Sunday morning some 30 years ago, while I was serving in a stake presidency, we received a telephone call from one of our faithful bishops. He explained that his ward had grown so rapidly that he could no longer provide a meaningful calling to all worthy members. His plea to us was that we divide the ward. While waiting for such approval, we decided as a stake presidency that we would visit the ward and call all these wonderful, worthy brothers and sisters to be stake missionaries.

About the third person I visited was a young female student attending the local university. After chatting for a few moments, I issued the call to serve as a missionary. There was silence for a few moments. Then she said, "President, don't you know that I am not active in the Church?"

After a few moments of silence on my part, I said, "No, I did not know you were not active."

She answered, "I have not been active in the Church for years." Then she said, "Don't you know that when you have been inactive, it's not all that easy to come back?"

I responded, "No. Your ward starts at 9:00 a.m. You come into the chapel, and you are with us."

She answered, "No, it is not that easy. You worry about a lot of things. You worry if someone will greet you or if you will sit alone and unnoticed during the meetings. And you worry about whether you will be accepted and who your new friends will be."

With tears rolling down her cheeks, she continued, "I know that my mother and father have been praying for me for years to bring me back into the Church." Then after a moment of silence, she said, "For the last three months I have been praying to find the courage, the strength, and the way to come back into activity." Then she asked, "President, do you suppose this calling could be an answer to those prayers?"

My eyes started to water as I responded, "I believe the Lord has answered your prayers."

She not only accepted the call; she became a fine missionary. And I'm certain she brought much joy not only to herself but also to her parents and probably other family members. 🔖

"Man Down!"

President Henry B. Eyring

Now they were desirous that salvation should
be declared to every creature, for they could not bear that
any human soul should perish; yea, even the very thoughts
that any soul should endure endless torment did cause
them to quake and tremble.
—Mosiah 28:3

Almost all of us have seen a battlefield portrayed in a film or read the description in a story. Over the din of explosions and the shouts of soldiers, there comes a cry, "Man down!"

When that cry sounds, faithful fellow soldiers will move toward the sound. Another soldier or a medic will ignore danger and move to the injured comrade. And the man down will know that help will come. Whatever the risk, someone will run low or crawl to get there in time to protect and give aid. That is true in every band of men joined in a difficult and dangerous mission which they are determined to fulfill at any sacrifice. The histories of such groups are full of stories of those loyal men who were determined that no man would be left behind.

Here is one instance from an official account. During fighting in Somalia in October of 1993, two United States Army Rangers in a helicopter during the firefight learned that two other helicopters near them had fallen to the earth. The two rangers, in their relative safety aloft, learned by radio that no ground forces were available to rescue one of the downed aircrews. Growing numbers of the enemy were closing in on the crash site.

The two men watching from above volunteered to go down to the ground (the words they used on the radio were to "be inserted") to protect their critically wounded comrades. Their request was denied because the situation was so dangerous. They asked a second time. Permission was again denied. Only after their third request were they put down on the ground.

Armed only with their personal weapons, they fought their way to the crashed helicopter and the injured fliers. They moved through intense small arms fire as enemies converged on the crash site. They pulled the wounded from the wreckage. They put themselves in a perimeter around the wounded, placing themselves in the most dangerous positions. They protected their comrades until their ammunition was depleted and they were fatally wounded. Their bravery and their sacrifice saved the life of a pilot who would have been lost.

They were each awarded posthumously the Medal of Honor, their nation's highest recognition for bravery in the face of an armed enemy. The citation reads that what they did was "above and beyond the call of duty."

But I wonder if they saw it that way as they moved to the downed airmen. Out of loyalty they felt a duty to stand by their fellow soldiers, whatever the cost. The courage to act and their selfless service came from feeling that they were responsible for the lives, the happiness, and the safety of comrades.

Such a feeling of responsibility for others is at the heart of faithful priesthood service. Our comrades are being wounded in the spiritual conflict around us. So are the people we are called to serve and protect from harm. Spiritual wounds are not easily visible, except with inspired eyes. ♙

A Critical Crossroad

President James E. Faust

The keeper of the gate is the Holy One of Israel; and he employeth
no servant there; and there is none other way save it be by the gate;
for he cannot be deceived, for the Lord God is his name.
—*2 Nephi 9:41*

In the fateful war year of 1942, I was inducted into the United States Army Air Corps. One cold night at Chanute Field, Illinois, I was given all-night guard duty. As I walked around my post, I meditated and pondered the whole miserable, long night through. By morning I had come to some firm conclusions. I was engaged to be married and knew that I could not support my wife on a private's pay. In a day or two, I filed my application for Officer's Candidate School. Shortly thereafter, I was summoned before the board of inquiry. My qualifications were few, but I had had two years of college and had finished a mission for the Church in South America.

The questions asked of me at the officers' board of inquiry took a very surprising turn. Nearly all of them centered upon my beliefs. "Do you smoke?" "Do you drink?" "What do you think of others who smoke and drink?" I had no trouble answering these questions.

"Do you pray?" "Do you believe that an officer should pray?" The officer asking these questions was a hard-bitten career soldier. He did not look like he prayed very often. I pondered. Would I give him offense if I answered how I truly believed? I wanted to be an officer very much so that I would not have to do all-night guard duty and KP and clean latrines, but mostly so my sweetheart and I could afford to be married.

I decided not to equivocate. I admitted that I did pray and that I felt that officers might seek divine guidance as some truly great generals had done. I told them that I thought that officers should be prepared to lead their men in all appropriate activities, if the occasion required, including prayer.

More interesting questions came. "In times of war, should not the moral code be relaxed? Does not the stress of battle justify men in doing things that they would not do when at home under normal situations?"

I recognized that here was a chance perhaps to make some points and look broad-minded. I suspected that the men who were asking me this question did not live by the standards that I had been taught. The thought flashed through my mind that perhaps I could say that I had my own beliefs, but I did not wish to impose them on others. But there seemed to flash before my mind the faces of the many people to whom I had taught the law of chastity as a missionary. In the end I simply said, "I do not believe there is a double standard of morality."

I left the hearing resigned to the fact that these hard-bitten officers would not like the answers I had given to their questions and would surely score me very low. A few days later when the scores were posted, to my astonishment, I had passed. I was in the first group taken for Officer's Candidate School! I graduated, became a second lieutenant, married my sweetheart, and we have "lived together happily ever after."

This was one of the critical crossroads of my life. Not all of the experiences in my life turned out that way or the way I wanted them to, but they have always been strengthening to my faith. 🔑

Elder Bradley D. Foster

They had been taught by their mothers, that if they did not doubt,
God would deliver them. And they rehearsed unto me the words
of their mothers, saying: We do not doubt our mothers knew it.
—Alma 56:47–48

By divine design, nurturing seems to be part of the spiritual heritage given to women. I've seen it in my daughters, and now I see it in my grand-daughters—even before they could walk, they wanted to carry and care for their little baby dolls.

In my profession as a farmer and a rancher, I've had a front-row seat to observe how a mother's natural affection manifests itself even in nature. Each spring we take a herd of cows and their new calves up along Idaho's Snake River, where they graze in the foothills for a month or so. Then we round them up and bring them down a road that leads to the corral. From there they are loaded onto trucks that carry them to their summer pastures in Montana.

On one particularly hot spring day, I was helping with the roundup by riding at the back of the herd as it moved down the dusty road toward the corral. My job was to gather any calves that had wandered from the road. The pace was slow and provided me some time to think.

Because it was so hot, the little calves kept running off into the trees to find shade. My thoughts turned to the youth of the Church who are sometimes distracted from the strait and narrow path. I also thought about those who have left the Church or who may feel that the Church has left their hearts while they were distracted. I thought to myself that a distraction doesn't have to be evil to be effective—sometimes it can just be shade.

After several hours of gathering up stray calves and with sweat running down my face, I yelled to the calves in frustration, "Just follow your mothers! They know where they're going! They've been down this road before!" Their mothers knew that even though the road was hot and dusty now, the end would be better than the beginning.

As soon as we got the herd into the corral, we noticed that three of the cows were pacing nervously at the gate. They could not find their calves and seemed to sense they were back on the road somewhere. One of the cowboys asked me what we should do. I

said, "I bet I know where those calves are. Back a quarter of a mile or so, there's a stand of trees. I'm sure we'll find them there."

Sure enough, just as I had suspected, we found our lost calves taking a nap in the shade. Our approach startled them, and they resisted our efforts to round them up. They were frightened because we were *not* their mothers! The more we tried to push them toward the corral, the more stubborn they became. Finally I said to the cowboys, "I'm sorry. I know better than this. Let's ride back and let their mothers out of the corral. The cows will come and get their calves, and the calves will follow their mothers." I was right. The mother cows knew exactly where to go to find their calves, and they led them back to the corral, as I had expected. 🐎

Basketball and Missionary Work

Elder Daryl H. Garn

There was a space granted unto man in which he might repent; therefore
this life became a probationary state; a time to prepare to meet God.
—Alma 12:24

When I was a young boy, my greatest desire was to play basketball. Fortunately, I had a father who was anxious to see that his son's desire was met. Dad and I would practice the basics of passing and dribbling the basketball hour after hour in our small kitchen. I would listen to college basketball games on the radio and dream of playing college ball someday. Serving a mission was far from my mind at that time; consequently, I spent very little effort in missionary preparation. In an attempt to ensure some balance in my life, my dad—who had not held a Church calling in many years—accepted the call to serve as my Scoutmaster. He operated by the book, and due to his diligence, some of my friends and I became Eagle Scouts. I realize now that Scouting is great preparation for a mission.

My boyhood dream came true when I made the basketball team at Utah State University. During my second year at Utah State, a returned missionary befriended me. Because of his example I began looking at my associates at school, including those on the basketball team, and realized that the people I most wanted to be like were those who had served missions. With the kind and loving mentoring of my good friend—and, I am sure, as a result of my mother's prayers and good example—my desires changed. After my second year at Utah State, I was called to serve in the Western Canadian Mission.

Three months into my mission, a new missionary from Idaho was assigned to be my companion. We had been together only a few days when I realized something very significant: my new companion knew the gospel, while I only knew the discussions. How I wished that I had prepared to be a missionary as hard as I had prepared to be a basketball player. My companion had prepared for his mission throughout his life and was immediately a valuable member of the team. How important it is for fathers and sons to work together on the basics in preparing for a mission.

I believe it is appropriate to compare the game of basketball to missionary work. The game of basketball includes not only the time you compete with another team on the court but also the hours of proper training and practice. The great work of saving souls is not limited to the two years that you serve a mission but, rather, requires years of righteous living and preparation in order to meet the standard for full-time missionary service.

ELDER JOHN H. GROBERG

Who shall ascend into the hill of the Lord? or who shall stand in
his holy place? He that hath clean hands, and a pure heart.
—Psalm 24:3–4

In His love for us, God has decreed that any worthy man, regardless of wealth, education, color, cultural background, or language, may hold His priesthood. Thus, any properly ordained man who is clean in hand, heart, and mind can connect with the unlimited power of the priesthood. I learned this lesson well as a young missionary years ago in the South Pacific.

My first assignment was to a small island hundreds of miles from headquarters, where no one spoke English, and I was the only white man. I was given a local companion named Feki who was then serving a building mission and was a priest in the Aaronic Priesthood.

After eight seasick days and nights on a small, smelly boat, we arrived at Niuatoputapu. I struggled with the heat, the mosquitoes, the strange food, culture, and language, as well as homesickness. One afternoon we heard cries of anguish and saw a family bringing the limp, seemingly lifeless body of their eight-year-old son to us. They wailed out that he had fallen from a mango tree and would not respond to anything. The faithful father and mother put him in my arms and said, "You have the Melchizedek Priesthood; bring him back to us whole and well."

Though my knowledge of the language was still limited, I understood what they wanted, and I was scared. I wanted to run away, but the expressions of love and faith that shone from the eyes of the parents and brothers and sisters kept me glued to the spot.

I looked expectantly at my companion. He shrugged and said, "I don't have the proper authority. You and the branch president hold the Melchizedek Priesthood." Grasping at that straw, I said, "Then this is the duty of the branch president."

No sooner had I said this than the branch president walked up. He had heard the commotion and returned from his garden. He was sweaty and covered with dirt and mud. I turned and explained what had happened and tried to give the young boy to him. He stepped back and said, "I will go and wash and put on clean clothes; then we will bless him and see what God has to say."

In near panic, I cried, "Can't you see? He needs help now!"

He calmly replied: "I know he needs a blessing. When I have washed myself and put on clean clothes, I will bring consecrated oil, and we will approach God and see what His will is. I cannot—I will not—approach God with dirty hands and muddy clothes." He turned and left me holding the boy. I was speechless.

Finally he returned, clean in body and dress and, I sensed, in heart as well. "Now," he said, "I am clean, so we will approach the throne of God."

That marvelous Tongan branch president, with clean hands and a pure heart, gave a beautiful and powerful priesthood blessing. I felt more like a witness than a participant. The words of the Psalmist came to my mind: "Who shall ascend into the hill of the Lord? . . . He that hath clean hands, and a pure heart" (Psalm 24:3–4). On that tiny island a worthy priesthood holder ascended into the hill of the Lord, and the power of the priesthood came down from heaven and authorized a young boy's life to continue.

...ng from his eyes, the branch president told me what to ...fort was required, but on the third day that little eight-...nited with his family.

...feel these truths. This was a tiny island in the midst ...icity, no hospital, no doctors—but none of that mat-...ove and faith, there was a branch president who held ...o understood the importance of cleanliness of hand ...ssion in cleanliness of body and dress, who exercised ...hood in righteousness and purity according to the will of God. That day his individual power *in* the priesthood was sufficient to connect with the unlimited power *of* the priesthood over earthly life.

When I look into the heavens at night and contemplate the endless galaxies therein, I am amazed at what a tiny dot our little earth is and how infinitesimally small I am. Yet I do not feel afraid, alone, insignificant, or distant from God. For I have witnessed His priesthood power connecting with clean hands and pure hearts on a tiny island in a vast ocean.

"I Could Have
Served a Mission"

ELDER
C. SCOTT GROW

That which shall be written . . .
shall grow together, unto the
confounding of false doctrines and
laying down of contentions,
and establishing peace among
the fruit of thy loins.
—2 Nephi 3:12

ecently, a member in Monterrey, Mexico, told me how the Book of Mormon changed his life. As a teenager, Jesús Santos was impressed by the LDS missionaries he saw walking down the dusty streets. He wanted to talk to them about their church but was told by a friend that you have to wait for them to contact you.

Many times he would go to the Church building and look through the iron fence at the missionaries and the Mutual youth playing games. They seemed to be so wholesome, and he wanted to be part of them. He would lean his chin on the fence, hoping that they would notice him and invite him to participate with them. It never happened.

As Jesús recounted his story to me, he said, "It is sad. I was a young man and could have served a full-time mission."

He moved to Monterrey, Mexico. Nine years later he was visiting a friend across town when the missionaries knocked at the door. His friend wanted to send them away. Jesús begged him to let the missionaries talk to them for just two minutes. His friend consented. The missionaries talked about the Book of Mormon, how Lehi's family traveled from Jerusalem to the Americas, and how the resurrected Jesus Christ visited Lehi's descendants in America.

Jesús wanted to know more. He was especially intrigued by the picture depicting

Christ's appearance in America. He gave the missionaries his address. He waited for months, but they never made contact with him.

Three more years passed. Some friends invited his family to a family home evening. They gave him a copy of the Book of Mormon.

As soon as he began to read it, he knew the Book of Mormon was true. Finally, 12 years after he first became aware of the Church, he and his wife were baptized. So many years had been lost. If missionaries had just talked to him, if the Mutual youth had just noticed a lonely teenager looking over the fence, if the missionaries in Monterrey had found him at home, his life would have been different during those 12 years. Gratefully, member neighbors invited him for a family home evening and shared with him that book which has such great converting power, the Book of Mormon. Today Jesús Santos serves as the president of the Monterrey Mexico Temple. 🐚

Sounding a
Perfect "A"

ELDER DAVID B. HAIGHT

And the church did meet together oft, to fast and to pray, and to speak one
with another concerning the welfare of their souls.
—Moroni 6:5

A few years ago, when Arturo Toscanini was musical director of the New York Philharmonic Orchestra in New York City, he had a Saturday afternoon radio broadcast. And one day he received in his mail a crumpled little note on some brownish paper which read:

"Dear Mr. Toscanini, I am a lonely sheepherder in the mountains of Wyoming. I have two prized possessions: an old violin and a battery radio. And the batteries are getting weak and beginning to run down on my radio, and my violin is so out of tune I can't play it anymore. Would you please sound an A next Saturday on your program?"

The next week on the program, Arturo Toscanini announced: "To a newfound friend in the mountains of Wyoming, the New York Philharmonic Orchestra is now, all together and in unison, going to sound a perfect A." And they sounded the perfect A. Then that lonely little man was able to tune the A string and then the E string and the D and the G from that perfect A.

Isn't it interesting to reflect in our own lives and in the lives of the many people—those whose violin or lives may be a little out of tune—that we are able to come to a general conference of the Church and hear the marvelous messages that are spoken? Those of us who have the opportunity to speak in conference pray mightily that we would have the energy and the strength and the vitality even as I do, as I enter the twilight of my life, to stand and bear witness of the truthfulness of this work—because I am a witness of it. 🔖

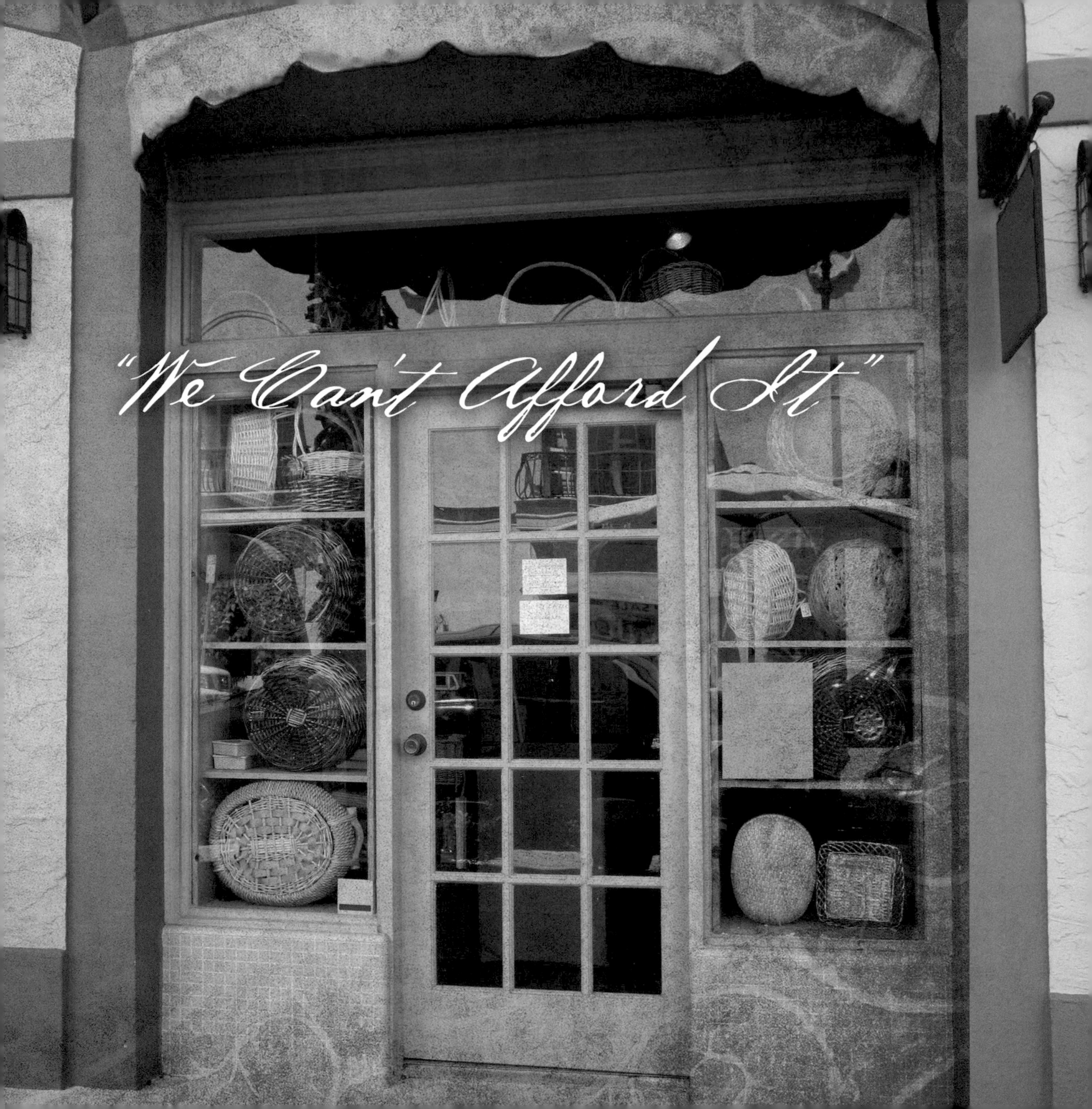
"We Can't Afford It"

Elder Robert D. Hales

Lay not up for yourselves treasures upon earth, where moth and rust doth corrupt, and where thieves break through and steal: but lay up for yourselves treasures in heaven, where neither moth nor rust doth corrupt, and where thieves do not break through nor steal.

—Matthew 6:19–20

I learned an important lesson from my wife when we were newly married and had very little money. I was in the air force, and we had missed Christmas together. I was on assignment overseas. When I got home, I saw a beautiful dress in a store window and suggested to my wife that if she liked it, we would buy it. Mary went into the dressing room of the store. After a moment the salesclerk came out, brushed by me, and returned the dress to its place in the store window. As we left the store, I asked, "What happened?" She replied, "It was a beautiful dress, but we can't afford it!" Those words went straight to my heart. I have learned that the three most loving words are "I love you," and the four most caring words for those we love are "We can't afford it."

A second lesson was learned several years later when we were more financially secure. Our wedding anniversary was approaching, and I wanted to buy Mary a fancy coat to show my love and appreciation for our many happy years together. When I asked what she thought of the coat I had in mind, she replied with words that again

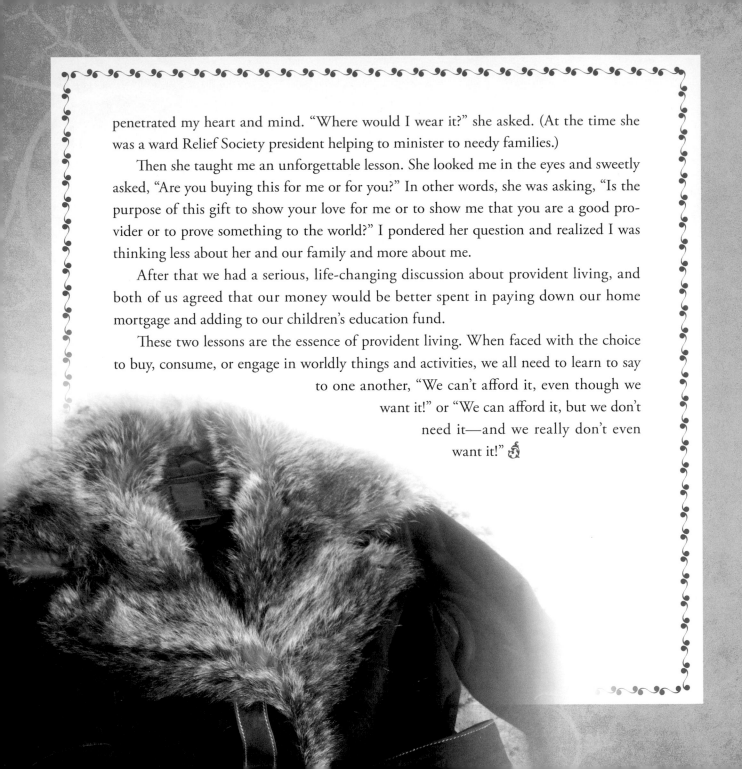

penetrated my heart and mind. "Where would I wear it?" she asked. (At the time she was a ward Relief Society president helping to minister to needy families.)

Then she taught me an unforgettable lesson. She looked me in the eyes and sweetly asked, "Are you buying this for me or for you?" In other words, she was asking, "Is the purpose of this gift to show your love for me or to show me that you are a good provider or to prove something to the world?" I pondered her question and realized I was thinking less about her and our family and more about me.

After that we had a serious, life-changing discussion about provident living, and both of us agreed that our money would be better spent in paying down our home mortgage and adding to our children's education fund.

These two lessons are the essence of provident living. When faced with the choice to buy, consume, or engage in worldly things and activities, we all need to learn to say to one another, "We can't afford it, even though we want it!" or "We can afford it, but we don't need it—and we really don't even want it!" 🖎

And now, behold, because ye have tried
the experiment, and planted the seed, and it
swelleth and sprouteth, and beginneth to grow,
ye must needs know that the seed is good.
—Alma 32:33

Planting Seeds of Faith

tightly against mine for warmth and security against the night. As I looked at my son beside me, suddenly I felt a surge of love pass through my body with such force that it pushed tears to my eyes. And, at that precise moment, he put his little arms around me and said, "Dad."

"Yes, son."

"Are you awake?"

"Yes, my son, I am awake."

"Dad, I love you a million, trillion times!"

And immediately he was asleep. But I was awake far into the night, expressing my great thanks for such wonderful blessings clothed with a little boy's body.

Now my son is a man with a son of his own. Once in a while the three of us go fishing. I look at my little red-headed grandson beside his father, and I see in my mind's eye the image of that wonderful moment long ago. The question so innocently asked, "Dad, are you awake?" still rings in my heart.

To every father, I pose the same penetrating question, "Dad, are you awake?" Do your sons ever wonder if you are asleep when it comes to the things that are most important to them? I would suggest that there are several areas that would indicate whether we are "awake" or "asleep" in the eyes of our sons. ❧

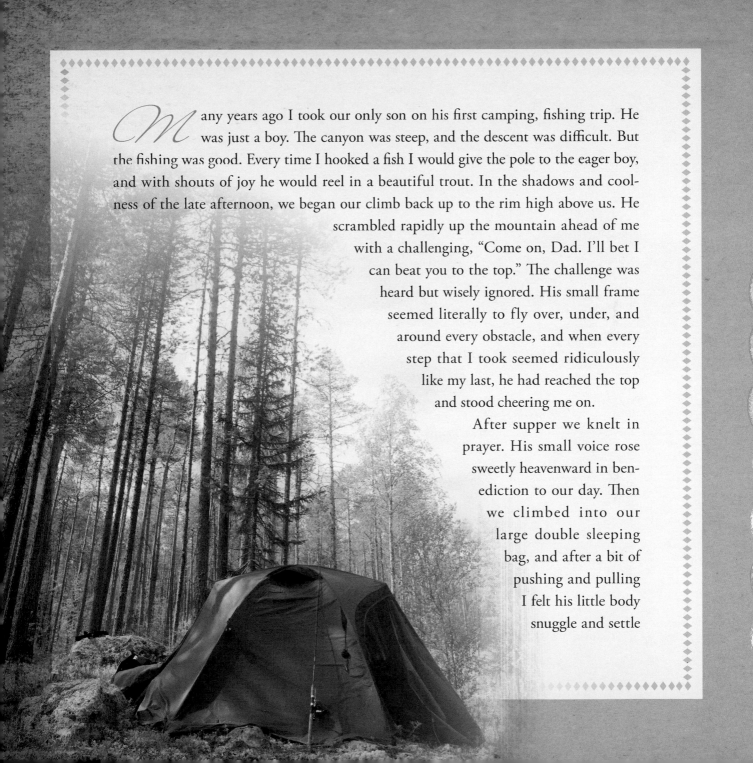

Many years ago I took our only son on his first camping, fishing trip. He was just a boy. The canyon was steep, and the descent was difficult. But the fishing was good. Every time I hooked a fish I would give the pole to the eager boy, and with shouts of joy he would reel in a beautiful trout. In the shadows and coolness of the late afternoon, we began our climb back up to the rim high above us. He scrambled rapidly up the mountain ahead of me with a challenging, "Come on, Dad. I'll bet I can beat you to the top." The challenge was heard but wisely ignored. His small frame seemed literally to fly over, under, and around every obstacle, and when every step that I took seemed ridiculously like my last, he had reached the top and stood cheering me on.

After supper we knelt in prayer. His small voice rose sweetly heavenward in benediction to our day. Then we climbed into our large double sleeping bag, and after a bit of pushing and pulling I felt his little body snuggle and settle

"Dad, Are You Awake?"

ELDER F. MELVIN HAMMOND

Arise from the dust, my sons, and be men,
and be determined in one mind and in one
heart, united in all things.

—2 Nephi 1:21

ELDER MARION D. HANKS

Some years ago a young sister missionary shared with me some of the circumstances of her call. Her humble father, a farmer, had willingly sacrificed much for the Lord and his kingdom. He was already sustaining two sons on missions when he talked with his daughter one day about her unexpressed desires to be a missionary and explained to her how the Lord had helped him to prepare to help her. He had gone to the fields to talk with the Lord, to tell him that he had no more material possessions to sell or sacrifice or to use as collateral for borrowing. He needed to know how he could help his daughter go on a mission. The Lord, he said, told him to plant onions. He thought he had misunderstood. Onions would not likely grow in this climate, others were not growing onions, he had no experience growing onions. After wrestling with the Lord for a time, he was again told to plant onions. So he borrowed money, purchased seeds, planted and nurtured and prayed. The elements were tempered, the onion crop prospered. He sold the crop, paid his debts to the bank and the government and the Lord, and put the remainder in an account under her name—enough to supply her wants on a mission.

I will not forget the story or the moment or the tears in her eyes or the sound of her voice or the feeling in me as she said, "Brother Hanks, I don't have any trouble believing in a loving Heavenly Father who knows my needs and will help me according to his wisdom if I am humble enough. I have a father just like that."

The Call to Serve

Offer the sacrifices of righteousness,
and put your trust in the Lord.
—Psalm 4:5

ELDER HAROLD G. HILLAM

I had [an interview] with a handsome zone leader in the Brazil São Paulo Interlagos Mission. I said to the missionary, "Tell me about your family." He then relayed the following. He was born into a wealthy family. His father had a responsible position in a multinational corporation. They moved from Brazil to Venezuela. He was one of seven children, all members of the Church.

When the missionary was fifteen years old, his father was shot and killed by a fleeing thief. In a family council it was decided to return to Brazil and invest their savings in the purchase of a small home. A year and a half later, the mother informed the children that she had been diagnosed with cancer. The family used valuable savings to help pay the medical expenses—but to no avail. Six months later the mother passed away, leaving the young family alone.

Our young missionary, Elder Bugs (pronounced Boogs), now sixteen years old, went to work, first selling clothing, then later computer supplies. He used his hard-earned money to support the young family. He said, "We were always blessed to have enough to eat. I would work during the day, then help the children with their studies at night. I especially miss my little sister. I taught her to read."

Elder Bugs continued, "Then the bishop invited me to come in for an interview. He called me on a mission. I told him I would need to speak with my family first. In our family council, they reminded me that Dad had always taught us that we should be prepared to serve the Lord as full-time missionaries. I accepted the call. When I received my letter from the prophet, I withdrew all my savings. I bought a new suit, a pair of pants, white shirts and ties, and a new pair of shoes. I gave the rest of the money to the bishop (enough for about four months of support for the family). I hugged my little family and left for my mission."

I looked at that brave young man and I said, "But, Elder, with you away, who is taking care of your family?"

"Oh," he said, "my brother is sixteen. He is the same age I was when our mother died. He is taking care of the family now."

I had an opportunity recently to talk by telephone with Elder Bugs. He has been home from his mission for six months now. When I asked him how he was doing, he said, "I have a good job again and I am caring for the family, but oh, how I miss my mission. It was the greatest thing I have ever done. I am now helping my younger brother prepare for his mission."

Why have these great missionaries and others like them been willing to sacrifice the comforts of home, family, loved ones, and sweethearts to answer the call to serve? It's because they have a testimony of Jesus Christ. And when they know Him, there is no bed too short or too hard, no climate too hot or too cold, no food too different or language so strange that they are unwilling to serve Him. No sacrifice is too great to serve the Master, who sacrificed His all to provide the way for His brothers and sisters to return home to their Heavenly Father. And because missionaries are faithful to their callings, thousands will revere their names throughout the eternities. 🔥

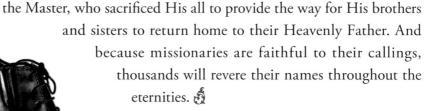

Following the Crowd

PRESIDENT GORDON B. HINCKLEY

*Therefore, I would that ye should be steadfast and immovable,
always abounding in good works, that Christ,
the Lord God Omnipotent, may seal you his.*
—Mosiah 5:15

The year we enrolled in junior high school the building could not accommodate all the students, so our class of the seventh grade was sent back to the Hamilton School [where we had attended elementary school].

We were insulted. We were furious. We'd spent six unhappy years in that building, and we felt we deserved something better. The boys of the class all met after school. We decided we wouldn't tolerate this kind of treatment. We were determined we'd go on strike.

The next day we did not show up. But we had no place to go. We couldn't stay home, because our mothers would ask questions. We didn't think of going downtown to a show. We had no money for that. We didn't think of going to the park. We were afraid we might be seen by Mr. Clayton, the truant officer. We didn't think of going out behind the school fence and telling shady stories because we didn't know any. We'd never heard of such things as drugs or anything of the kind. We just wandered about and wasted the day.

The next morning, the principal, Mr. Stearns, was at the front door of the school to greet us. His demeanor matched his name. He said some pretty straightforward things and then told us that we could not come back to school until we brought a note from our parents. That was my first experience with a lockout. Striking, he said, was not the way to settle a problem. We were expected to be responsible citizens, and if we had a complaint, we could come to the principal's office and discuss it.

There was only one thing to do, and that was to go home and get the note.

I remember walking sheepishly into the house. My mother asked what was wrong. I told her. I said that I needed a note. She wrote a note. It was very brief. It was the most stinging rebuke she ever gave me. It read as follows:

"Dear Mr. Stearns,

"Please excuse Gordon's absence yesterday. His action was simply an impulse to follow the crowd."

She signed it and handed it to me.

I walked back over to school and got there about the same time a few other boys did. We all handed our notes to Mr. Stearns. I do not know whether he read them, but I have never forgotten my mother's note. Though I had been an active party to the action we had taken, I resolved then and there that I would never do anything on the basis of simply following the crowd. I determined then and there that I would make my own decisions on the basis of their merits and my standards and not be pushed in one direction or another by those around me.

That decision has blessed my life many times, sometimes in very uncomfortable circumstances. It has kept me from doing some things which, if indulged in, could at worst have resulted in serious injury and trouble, and at the best would have cost me my self-respect. 🖋

The Lord Sent an Angel

ELDER JEFFREY R. HOLLAND

I will not leave you comfortless: I will come to you.
—John 14:18

May I share with you an account by my friend and BYU colleague, the late Clyn D. Barrus. I do so with the permission of his wife, Marilyn, and their family.

Referring to his childhood on a large Idaho farm, Brother Barrus spoke of his nightly assignment to round up the cows at milking time. Because the cows pastured in a field bordered by the occasionally treacherous Teton River, the strict rule in the Barrus household was that during the spring flood season the children were never to go after any cows who ventured across the river. They were always to return home and seek mature help.

One Saturday just after his seventh birthday, Brother Barrus's parents promised the family a night at the movies if the chores were done on time. But when young Clyn arrived at the pasture, the cows he sought had crossed the river, even though it was running at high flood stage. Knowing his rare night at the movies was in jeopardy, he decided to go after the cows himself, even though he had been warned many times never to do so.

As the seven-year-old urged his old horse, Banner, down into the cold, swift stream, the horse's head barely cleared the water. An adult sitting on the horse would have been safe, but at Brother Barrus's tender age, the current completely covered him except when the horse lunged forward several times, bringing Clyn's head above water just enough to gasp for air.

Here I turn to Brother Barrus's own words:

"When Banner finally climbed the other bank, I realized that my life had been in grave danger and that I had done a terrible thing—I had knowingly disobeyed my father. I felt that I could redeem myself only by bringing the cows home safely. Maybe then my father would forgive me. But it was already dusk, and I didn't know for sure where I was. Despair overwhelmed me. I was wet and cold, lost and afraid.

"I climbed down from old Banner, fell to the ground by his feet, and began to cry. Between thick sobs, I tried to offer a prayer, repeating over and over to my Father in Heaven, 'I'm sorry. Forgive me! I'm sorry. Forgive me!'

"I prayed for a long time. When I finally looked up, I saw through my tears a figure dressed in white walking toward me. In the dark, I felt certain it must be an angel sent in answer to my prayers. I did not move or make a sound as the figure approached, so overwhelmed was I by what I saw. Would the Lord really send an angel to me, who had been so disobedient?

"Then a familiar voice said, 'Son, I've been looking for you.' In the darkness I recognized the voice of my father and ran to his outstretched arms. He held me tightly, then said gently, 'I was worried. I'm glad I found you.'

"I tried to tell him how sorry I was, but only disjointed words came out of my trembling lips—'Thank you . . . darkness . . . afraid . . . river . . . alone.' Later that night I learned that when I had not returned from the pasture, my father had come looking for me. When neither I nor the cows were to be found, he knew I had crossed the river and was in danger. Because it was dark and time was of the essence, he removed his clothes down to his long white thermal underwear, tied his shoes around his neck, and swam a treacherous river to rescue a wayward son."

I testify of angels, both the heavenly and the mortal kind. In doing so I am testifying that God never leaves us alone, never leaves us unaided in the challenges that we face. "[Nor] will he, so long as time shall last, or the earth shall stand, or there shall be one man [or woman or child] upon the face thereof to be saved" (Moroni 7:36). On occasions, global or personal, we may feel we are distanced from God, shut out from heaven, lost, alone in dark and dreary places. Often enough that distress can be of our own making, but even then the Father of us all is watching and assisting. And always there are those angels who come and go all around us, seen and unseen, known and unknown, mortal and immortal.

"You Didn't Call Me"

ELDER F. BURTON HOWARD

*Yea, and they did obey and observe to perform
every word of command with exactness.*
—Alma 57:21

When my wife and I were first married, my parents lived in another state. During a break in our university schedule, we decided to go visit them. We made sandwiches, packed the car, prepared a bed in the backseat for our young son so that he could rest during the 10-hour trip. After a full day in the car, we were beginning to get on each other's nerves. The preschooler never slept and seemed to gather energy as the day wore on. We knew that if he would just close his eyes and be quiet for a while, he would fall asleep.

After sundown, with two hours of travel still to go, we decided to play a game. The purpose of the game was to try to get an exhausted youngster to sleep. We called it hide-and-seek. Have you ever tried to play hide-and-seek in a car? Let me tell you how we did it. We said to the small boy in back, "Let's play hide-and-seek." He enthusiastically agreed. We said, "Close your eyes and don't open them until we call you. We need time to hide."

The game started. A front-seat passenger would crouch down in the seat and 10 or 15 seconds later would call, "OK." Our son would bound over the seat and say, "Aha, I found you!" We would say, "Next time we will hide better. Close your eyes again." A minute or more would go by. Then we would call, and again he would energetically climb over the seat to find us. Finally we said, "We have a really good place to hide this time. It will take longer. Close your eyes and we will call you."

A minute, two minutes, five minutes went by. We drove along in silence. The tranquility was marvelous. We must have traveled 15 miles before we began to whisper quiet congratulations to ourselves on the success of our devious game.

Then, from out of the backseat, came the sobbing voice of a heartbroken little boy. "You didn't call me, and you said you would."

"You didn't do what you agreed to do." What a terrible accusation. It was a defining moment in our lives. We knew that we could never play that game again. 🔖

Happiness
at 3:30 a.m.

SISTER KATHLEEN H. HUGHES

But unto him that keepeth my commandments
I will give the mysteries of my kingdom, and
the same shall be in him a well of living water,
springing up unto everlasting life.
—D&C 63:23

I remember the day a dear family friend passed away. Lucile was 89 years old and had been a widow for more than 20 years. She was not a rich woman, she was not famous, and most of the world knew nothing of her passing. But her family knew. Her neighbors knew. The members of her ward knew. For all who had experienced her love, her death had left the world a diminished place.

During her years as a widow, Lucile had endured difficult challenges, including the death of a beloved grandson and infirmities brought on by age. But Lucile continued to nourish everyone she knew with her spirit; with her baked goods, quilts, and afghans;

with her humor and goodwill. And she loved to work in the temple. One spring day in 1981, she wrote in her journal: "This morning at 3:30 a.m., as I was walking up the path to the temple, I watched the flag gently blowing in the breeze and looked at the beautiful sky and thought how happy I was to be there. I felt sad for all the people who [were] sleeping and missing the awakening of a beautiful day."

Most of us don't think the world is "awakening" at 3:30 in the morning, and we're perfectly happy to roll over in bed about then and allow Lucile to feel sorry for us. But what an attitude! Only a flow of goodness from within could explain it. Did she possess this purity of spirit at 15, at 25, or even 55? I don't know. In most cases, it probably takes a lifetime of listening to the Holy Ghost before we know God's voice so well and before we trust in the living waters enough to taste them throughout the entire day—especially a day that begins at 3:30 a.m. But I believe the living waters sustained Lucile during those long years when she might have given way to self-pity, and her life, her spirit, became nourishment to everyone she knew. 🍃

"Is There Someone Who Can Teach Me?"

SISTER ELAINE L. JACK

He that preacheth and he that receiveth, understand one another,
and both are edified and rejoice together.
—D&C 50:22

Without question, those progressing eternally are those on the straight and narrow; they are spiritual and charitable. A bishop in the Dominican Republic exemplifies such a life. After sacrament meeting in his ward, a new convert approached him and said, "Bishop, I notice that the members are always looking at books when they sing. I want to do that. They look at books in Sunday School class. I want to do that." Quietly, the brother said, "Bishop, I want to be a good member. I want to do all the Lord's work. But I can't read. Is there someone who can teach me?"

"Yes," said the bishop. And then he tried to think of a likely tutor. He found himself saying, "I'll teach you to read."

For many months this new convert and his wife met weekly with the bishop. They learned to read using the scriptures. Now this was a busy bishop, like they all are. He could have delegated the responsibility, but the Spirit had prompted him to take the assignment. They became friends in the gospel as they studied together. After two years, the bishop was released and a new bishop called. Sustained to follow him as the leader of the ward was his student of the scriptures. This bishop set out to teach his friends how to read the gospel message; and in the process, he showed them how to live it. Could this bishop have seen the end when he began? How often do we follow the dictums of the Lord and in doing so influence eternity? 🐚

Seven Little Boys

*Be thou an example of the believers, in word, in conversation,
in charity, in spirit, in faith, in purity.*
—1 Timothy 4:12

President Spencer W. Kimball

Long years ago when I was in the stake presidency in the St. Joseph Stake in Arizona, one Sabbath day I filled an assignment in the Eden Ward. The building was a small one, and most of the people were sitting close to us as we sat on the raised platform about a foot and a half above the floor of the building itself.

As the meeting proceeded, my eye was attracted to seven little boys on the front seat of the chapel. I was delighted with seven little boys in this ward conference. I made a mental note, then shifted my interest to other things. Soon my attention was focused on the seven little boys again.

It seemed strange to me that each of the seven little fellows raised his right leg and put it over the left knee, and then in a moment all would change at the same time and put the left leg over the right knee. I thought it was unusual, but I just ignored it.

In a moment or two, all in unison would brush their hair with their right hands, and then all seven little boys leaned lightly on their wrists and supported their faces by their hands, and then simultaneously they went back to the crossing of their legs again.

It all seemed so strange, and I wondered about it as I was trying to think of what I was going to say in the meeting. And then all at once it came to me like a bolt of lightning. These boys were mimicking me!

That day I learned the lesson of my life—that we who are in positions of authority must be careful indeed, because others watch us and find in us their examples. ◊

ELDER JOHN R. LASATER

I am the good shepherd, and know my sheep, and am known of mine.
—John 10:14

Some years ago, it was my privilege to visit the country of Morocco as part of an official United States government delegation. As part of that visit, we were invited to travel some distance into the desert to visit some ruins. Five large black limousines moved across the beautiful Moroccan countryside at considerable speed. I was riding in the third limousine, which had lagged some distance behind the second. As we topped the brow of a hill, we noticed that the limousine in front of us had pulled off to the side of the road. As we drew nearer, I sensed that an accident had occurred and suggested to my driver that we stop. The scene before us has remained with me for these many years.

An old shepherd, in the long, flowing robes of the Savior's day, was standing near the limousine in conversation with the driver. Nearby, I noted a small flock of sheep numbering not more than fifteen or twenty. An accident *had* occurred. The king's vehicle had struck and injured one of the sheep belonging to the old shepherd. The driver of the vehicle was explaining to him the law of the land. Because the king's vehicle had injured one of the sheep belonging to the old shepherd, he was now entitled to one hundred times its value at maturity. However, under the same law, the injured sheep must be slain and the meat divided among the people. My interpreter hastily added, "But the old shepherd will not accept the money. They never do."

Startled, I asked him why. And he added, "Because of the love he has for each of his sheep." It was then that I noticed the old shepherd reach down, lift the injured lamb in his arms, and place it in a large pouch on the front of his robe. He kept stroking its head, repeating the same word over and over again. When I asked the meaning of the word, I was informed, "Oh, he is calling it by name. All of his sheep have a name, for he is their shepherd, and the good shepherds know each one of their sheep by name."

It was as my driver predicted. The money was refused, and the old shepherd with his small flock of sheep, with the injured one tucked safely in the pouch on his robe, disappeared into the beautiful deserts of Morocco.

As we continued our journey toward the ruins, my interpreter shared with me more of the traditions and practices of the shepherds of that land. Each evening at sundown, for example, the shepherds bring their small flocks of sheep to a common enclosure where they are secured against the wolves that roam the deserts of Morocco. A single shepherd then is employed to guard the gate until morning. Then the shepherds come to the enclosure one by one, enter therein, and call forth their sheep—by name. The sheep will not hearken unto the voice of a stranger but will leave the enclosure only in the care of their true shepherd, confident and secure because the shepherd knows their names and they know his voice. 🐑

Jesus saith to Simon Peter, Simon, son of Jonas, lovest thou me more than these? He saith unto him, Yea, Lord; thou knowest that I love thee. He saith unto him, Feed my lambs.
—John 21:15

The Summer of
the Lambs

SISTER JAYNE B. MALAN

The day school was out at the beginning of each summer, our family went to our ranch in Wyoming. It was there with my parents and brothers and sisters, and a few cousins mixed in, that I learned about family loyalty; love and concern; birth and death; that one must finish a job once it is started; and, to quote my father, "There are only two things important—the family and the Church."

One year my father was waiting for us as we arrived. He said he had a big job for my brother Clay and me to do that summer. I was about twelve at the time, and my brother was two years older. Pointing to the field by the side of the house, my father said, "Do you see all of these lambs in that field? I'll share the money we get for the ones you raise when we sell them in the fall." Well, we were excited. Not only did we have a significant job to do, but we were going to be rich! There were a lot of lambs in that field—about 350 of them. And all we had to do was feed them.

However, there was one thing that my father hadn't mentioned. None of the lambs had mothers. Just after shearing, there was a violent storm that chilled the newly shorn sheep. Dad lost a thousand ewes that year. The mothers of our lambs were among them.

To feed one or two baby animals is one thing, but to feed 350 is something else! It was hard. There was plenty of grass, but the lambs couldn't eat the grass. They didn't have teeth. They needed milk. So we made some long, V-shaped feeding troughs out of some boards. Then we got a great big tin washtub, ground up some grain, and added milk to make a thin mash. While my brother poured the mash into the troughs, I rounded up the lambs, herded them to the troughs, and said, "Eat!" Well, they just stood there looking at me. Although they were hungry and there was food in front of them, they still wouldn't eat. No one had taught them to drink milk out of a trough. So I tried pushing them toward the troughs. Do you know what happens when you try to push sheep? They run the other way. And when you lose one, you could lose them all because others will follow. That's the way with sheep.

We tried lining up the lambs along the troughs and pushing their noses down in the milk, hoping they'd get a taste and want some more. We tried wiggling our fingers in the milk to get them to suck on our fingers. Some of them would drink, but most of them ran away.

Many of the lambs were slowly starving to death. The only way we could be sure they were being fed was to pick them up in our arms, two at a time, and feed them like babies.

And then there were the coyotes. At night the coyotes would sit up on the hill, and they'd howl. The next morning we would see the results of their night's work, and we would have two or three more lambs to bury. The coyotes would sneak up on the lambs, scatter the herd, and then pick out the ones they wanted and go after them. The first were those that were weak or separated from the flock. Often in the night when the coyotes came and the lambs were restless, my dad would take out his rifle and shoot in the air to scare them away. We felt secure when my dad was home because we knew our lambs were safe when he was there to watch over them.

Clay and I soon forgot about being rich. All we wanted to do was save our lambs. The hardest part was seeing them die.

Every morning we would find five, seven, ten lambs that had died during the night. Some the coyotes got, and others starved to death surrounded by food they couldn't or wouldn't eat.

Part of our job was to gather up the dead lambs and help dispose of them. I got used to that, and it really wasn't so bad until I named one of the lambs. It was an awkward little thing with a black spot on its nose. It was always under my feet, and it knew my voice. I loved my lamb. It was one I held in my arms and fed with a bottle like a baby.

One morning my lamb didn't come when I called. I found it later that day under the willows by the creek. It was dead. With tears streaming down my face, I picked up my lamb and went to find my father. Looking up at him, I said, "Dad, isn't there someone who can help us feed our lambs?"

After a long moment he said, "Jayne, once a long, long time ago, someone else said almost those same words. He said, 'Feed my lambs. . . . Feed my sheep. . . . Feed my sheep'" (John 21:15–17). Dad put his arms around me and let me cry for a time, then went with me to bury my lamb.

It wasn't until many years later that I fully realized the meaning of my father's words. I was pondering the scripture in Moses that says, "For behold, this is my work and my glory—to bring to pass the immortality and eternal life of [all mankind]" (Moses 1:39). As I thought about the mission of the Savior, I remembered the summer of the lambs, and, for a few brief moments, I thought I could sense how the Savior must feel with so many lambs to feed, so many souls to save. 🐑

Ambition versus Hard Work

Thou shalt not be idle; for he that is idle shall not eat

the bread nor wear the garments of the laborer.

—D&C 42:42

Bishop Keith B. McMullin

A young man, full of ambition and energy, enrolled in a fine university. At the time, he was a priest in the Aaronic Priesthood. His goal was lofty—he wanted to become a doctor. His aim was ambitious—he wanted to be rich. He wanted to play football, so he sought out the coaches and eventually made the team. Now he could have the recognitions and bragging rights unique in the world of university sports. Such were the notions in his head.

But he had given little thought to something that would ultimately dismantle his lofty and vain ambitions—he had failed to lay up in store. He had overlooked the importance of adequate preparation, the requirements of regular attendance and disciplined study, and the college chemistry class. The consequence was swift and merciless. It took less than 90 days. It happened this way:

The day he found his 5-foot-8-inch, 170-pound body on the line of scrimmage opposite a mammoth lineman from the varsity squad, he knew he was in the wrong sport. Unaccustomed to rigorous study, his eyes and mind refused to function after a brief time in the books.

The capstone of defeat was the final chemistry exam. Suffice it to say that his random answers to multiple-choice questions did not even approximate the law of averages. He failed miserably.

Hard work, a mission that awakened in him a correct vision of life's purposes, and unrelenting preparation eventually overcame the consequence of this brief period of foolishness. Even today, however, I still have nightmares about that chemistry class.

President Thomas S. Monson

If ye do not watch yourselves, and your thoughts, and your words, and your deeds, and observe the commandments of God, and continue in the faith of what ye have heard concerning the coming of our Lord, even unto the end of your lives, ye must perish. And now, O man, remember, and perish not.
—Mosiah 4:30

On July 16, 1945, the USS *Indianapolis* departed the Mare Island Naval Shipyard in California on a secret cargo mission to Tinian Island in the Marianas. The cargo included highly sophisticated equipment which could well bring an end to the Second World War, with all its suffering, remorse, and death. The ship delivered its cargo on July 26 and was heading, unescorted, toward Leyte in the Philippines.

Because they were traveling through hostile waters in the Philippine Sea, the captain had discretionary orders to follow a zigzag course of travel to prevent detection by and attack from the enemy. He failed to do so. Just before midnight on Sunday, July 29, 1945, as the *Indianapolis* continued toward Leyte Gulf, the heavy cruiser was discovered by an enemy submarine. Easily avoiding detection while submerging to periscope depth, the submarine fired a fanwise salvo of six torpedoes from 1,500 yards.

As the torpedoes struck the target, explosions of ammunition and aviation fuel ripped away the cruiser's bow and destroyed its power center. Without power, the radio officer was unable to send a distress signal. The order to abandon ship, when it came, had to be passed by word of mouth because all communications were down. Just 12 minutes after being hit, the stern rose up a hundred feet straight into the air, and the ship plunged into the depths of the sea. Of the nearly 1,200-man crew, approximately 400 were killed instantly or went down with the ship. About 800 survived the sinking and went into the water.

Four days later, on August 2, 1945, the pilot of a Lockheed Ventura, flying on patrol, noticed an unusual oil slick on the water's surface and followed it for 15 miles. Then the plane's occupants spotted those men who had managed to survive since the *Indianapolis* had gone down. A major rescue effort began. Ships hurried to the area, and planes were dispatched to drop food, water, and survival gear to the men. Of the approximately 800 who had gone into the water, only 316 remained alive. The rest had been claimed by the perilous, shark-infested sea.

Two weeks later World War II was over. The sinking of the *Indianapolis*, called "the final great naval tragedy of World War II," is now legend.

Are there lessons for our lives in the horrific experience of those men aboard the *Indianapolis*?

They were in harm's way. Danger lurked; the enemy stalked. The vessel sailed on, disregarding the command to zigzag, and thus it became an easy target. Catastrophe was the result.

Our journey through mortality will at times place us in harm's way. Are we prepared for the voyage of life? The sea of life can at times become turbulent. Crashing waves of emotional conflict may break all around us. Chart your course, be cautious, and follow safety measures. In so doing, we will sail safely the seas of life and arrive at home port—even the celestial kingdom of God. 🙡

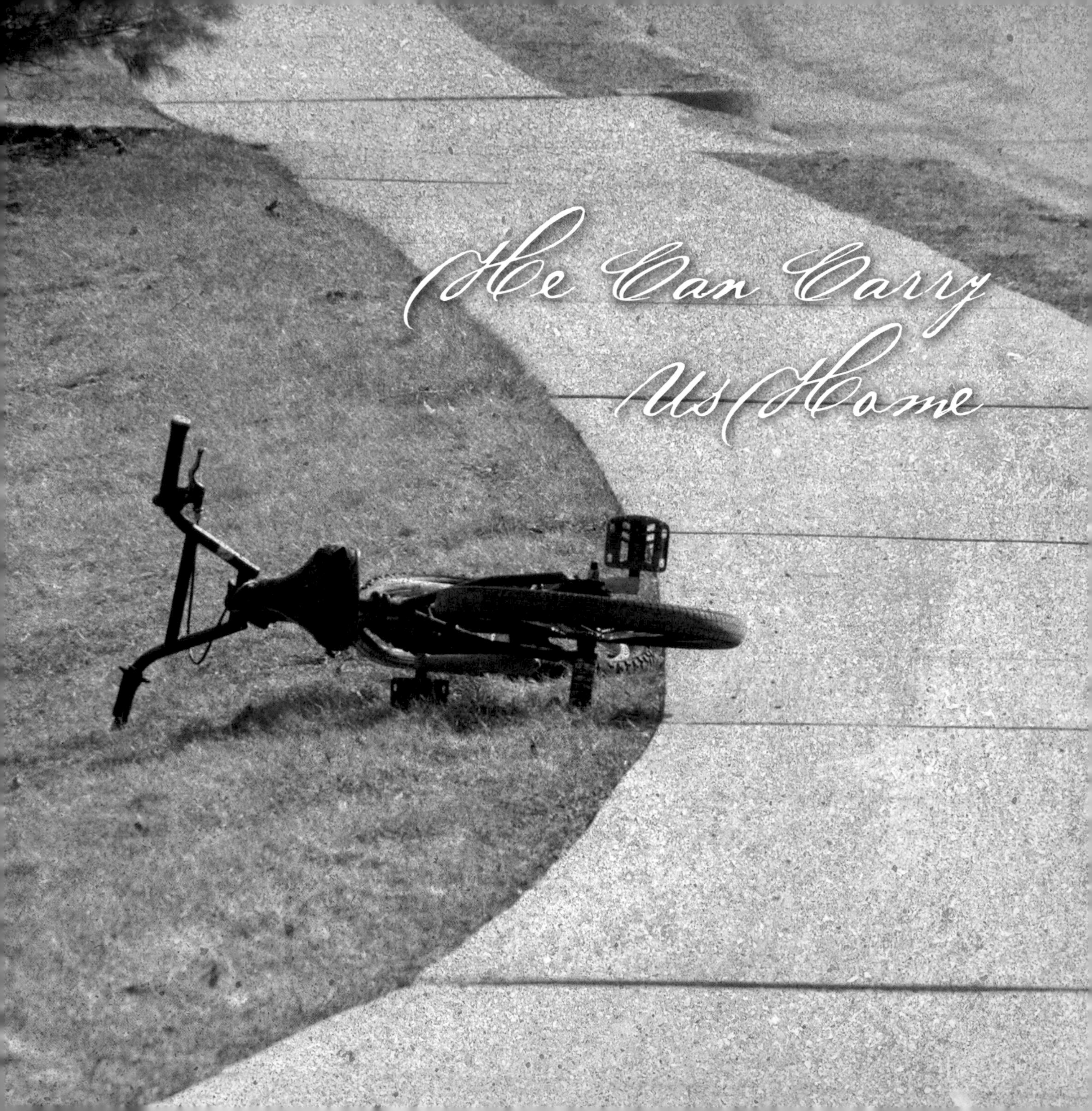
He Can Carry
Us Home

Sister Margaret D. Nadauld

And he will take upon him their infirmities, that his bowels may be filled with
mercy, according to the flesh, that he may know according
to the flesh how to succor his people according to their infirmities.
—Alma 7:12

A simple thing happened many years ago that I have always remembered because it caused me to think about the Savior's mission. Although it was just a childish incident, it has some meaning. It happened when our twins were only about five years old. They were just learning to ride their bicycles. As I glanced out the window, I saw them speeding down the street on their bikes going very fast! Perhaps they were going a little too fast for their level of ability, because all of a sudden Adam had a terrible crash! He was tangled up in the wreck, and all I could see was a twist of handlebars and tires and arms and legs. His little twin brother, Aaron, saw the whole thing happen, and immediately he skidded to a stop and jumped off his bike. He threw it down and ran to the aid of his brother, whom he loved very much. These little twins truly were of one heart. If one hurt, so did the other. If one got tickled, they both laughed. If one started a sentence, the other could complete it. What one felt, the other did also. So it was painful for Aaron to see Adam crash!

Adam was a mess. He had skinned knees, he was bleeding from a head wound, his pride was damaged, and he was crying. In a fairly gentle, five-year-old way, Aaron helped his brother get untangled from the crash, he checked out the wounds, and then he did the dearest thing. He picked his brother up and carried him home. Or tried to. This wasn't very easy because they were the same size, but he tried. And as he struggled and lifted and half-dragged, half-carried his brother along, they finally reached the front porch. By this time, Adam, the injured one, was no longer crying, but Aaron, the rescuer, was. When asked, "Why are you crying, Aaron?" he said simply, "Because Adam hurts." And so he had brought him home to help, home to someone who knew what to do, to someone who could cleanse the wounds, bind them up, and make it better—home to love.

Just as one twin helped his brother in need, so might we all be lifted, helped, even carried at times by our beloved Savior, the Lord Jesus Christ. He feels what we feel; He knows our heart. It was His mission to wipe away our tears, cleanse our wounds, and bless us with His healing power. He can carry us home to our Heavenly Father with the strength of His matchless love. 🦎

Navigating the Rough Rapids of Life

ELDER RUSSELL M. NELSON

They came and caught hold of the end of the rod of iron; and they did press their way forward, continually holding fast to the rod of iron, until they came forth and fell down and partook of the fruit of the tree.
—1 Nephi 8:30

Years ago when Sister Nelson and I had several teenaged daughters, we took our family on a vacation far away from telephones and boyfriends. We went on a raft trip down the Colorado River through the Grand Canyon. As we started our journey, we had no idea how dangerous this trip could be.

The first day was beautiful. But on the second day, when we approached Horn Creek rapids and saw that precipitous drop ahead, I was terrified. Floating on a rubber raft, our precious family was about to plunge over a waterfall! Instinctively I put one arm around my wife and the other around our youngest daughter. To protect them, I tried to hold them close to me. But as we reached the precipice, the bended raft became a giant sling and shot me into the air. I landed into the roiling rapids of the river. I had a hard time coming up. Each time I tried to find air, I hit the underside of the raft. My family couldn't see me, but I could hear them shouting, "Daddy! Where's Daddy?"

I finally found the side of the raft and rose to the surface. The family pulled my nearly drowned body out of the water. We were thankful to be safely reunited.

The next several days were pleasant and delightful. Then came the last day, when we were to go over Lava Falls, known as the most dangerous drop of the journey. When I saw what was ahead, I immediately asked to beach the raft and hold an emergency family council meeting, knowing that if we were to survive this experience, we needed to plan carefully. I reasoned with our family: "No matter what happens, the rubber raft will remain on top of the water. If we cling with all our might to ropes secured to the raft, we can make it. Even if the raft should capsize, we will be all right if we hang tightly to the ropes."

I turned to our little seven-year-old daughter and said, "All of the others will cling to a rope. But you will need to hold on to your daddy. Sit behind me. Put your arms around me and hold me tightly while I hold the rope."

That we did. We crossed those steep, rough rapids—hanging on for dear life—and all of us made it safely.

I nearly lost my life learning a lesson that I now give to you. As we go through life, even through very rough waters, a father's instinctive impulse to cling tightly to his wife or to his children may not be the best way to accomplish his objective. Instead, if he will lovingly cling to the Savior and the iron rod of the gospel, his family will want to cling to him and to the Savior.

This lesson is surely not limited to fathers. Regardless of gender, marital status, or age, individuals can choose to link themselves directly to the Savior, hold fast to the rod of His truth, and lead by the light of that truth. By so doing, they become examples of righteousness to whom others will want to cling. 🎣

"I Was Praying for Our Son"

Elder Brent H. Nielson

Even before they were born, they . . . were prepared to come forth in the due time of the Lord to labor in his vineyard for the salvation of the souls of men.
—D&C 138:56

On April 6, 1974, the Church sustained a new prophet, President Spencer W. Kimball. That same day I received my call to serve as a full-time missionary in Finland. I wasn't aware at the time that President Kimball had just delivered a landmark address that week to the General Authorities and regional representatives of the Church. Later I learned that in that address President Kimball prophetically outlined his vision as to how we as a Church would accomplish the Savior's charge to "teach all nations."

In his address, President Kimball invited the members of the Church to lengthen their stride and enlarge their vision. . . .

While serving in Finland, I learned that my mission president's wife, Sister Lea Mahoney, was a native of Finland. As a young girl she had grown up in the eastern portion of Finland in a city named Viipuri. As the ravages of war engulfed Finland and other countries during World War II, she and her family left their home and Viipuri became part of the Soviet Union and was renamed Vyborg. In our zone conferences, Sister Mahoney would tell us of those left behind in Viipuri and of her desire that the gospel be taken to them. Following President Kimball's challenge, we unitedly prayed that the hearts of the leaders of that nation would be softened so that the gospel could be taken by our missionaries into the Soviet Union.

We would go to the border between Finland and the Soviet Union and see the guard towers and the fences, and we would wonder who those brave young men and young women would be and when they would cross that border to take the gospel to the people there. I must admit, at that time it seemed like an impossible task.

Three years ago, our son Eric received a mission call to serve in the Russia St. Petersburg Mission. In his first letter home, he wrote something like this: "Dear Mom and Dad, I have been assigned to my first city in Russia. Dad, you may have heard of it before. It is called Vyborg, but it was previously a Finnish city named Viipuri."

Tears came to my eyes as I understood that Eric was in the very city we had prayed about 32 years earlier. Eric found a chapel there and a branch of faithful Saints. He was living and serving in a place that to me as a young man had seemed impossible to enter.

I did not realize those many years ago, as we prayed for the borders to open and the missionaries to go in, that I was praying for our son. Most important for you of the rising generation, our son Eric did not realize that he and his companions were the answer to the prayers that had been offered by thousands of faithful Saints so many years ago.

The Promise of Protection

ELDER DALLIN H. OAKS

He will preserve the righteous by his power, . . . wherefore, the righteous
need not fear; for thus saith the prophet, they shall be saved.
—*1 Nephi 22:17*

All over the world, faithful Latter-day Saints are protected from the powers of the evil one and his servants until they have finished their missions in mortality. For some the mortal mission is brief, as with some valiant young men who have lost their lives in missionary service. But for most of us the mortal journey is long, and we continue our course with the protection of guardian angels.

During my life I have had many experiences of being guided in what I should do and in being protected from injury and also from evil. The Lord's protecting care has shielded me from the evil acts of others and has also protected me from surrendering to my own worst impulses. I enjoyed that protection one warm summer night on the streets of Chicago. I have never shared this experience in public. I do so now because it is a persuasive illustration of my subject.

My wife, June, had attended a ward officers' meeting. When I came to drive her home, she was accompanied by a sister we would take home on our way. She lived in the nearby Woodlawn area, which was the territory of a gang called the Blackstone Rangers.

I parked at the curb outside this sister's apartment house and accompanied her into the lobby and up the stairs to her door. June remained in the car on 61st Street. She locked all of the doors, and I left the keys in the ignition in case she needed to drive away. We had lived on the south side of Chicago for quite a few years and were accustomed to such precautions.

Back in the lobby, and before stepping out into the street, I looked carefully in each direction. By the light of a nearby streetlight, I could see that the street was deserted except for three young men walking by. I waited until they were out of sight and then walked quickly toward our car.

As I came to the driver's side and paused for June to unlock the door, I saw one of these young men running back toward me. He had something in his right hand, and I knew what it would be. There was no time to get into the car and drive away before he came within range.

Fortunately, as June leaned across to open the door, she glanced through the back window and saw this fellow coming around the end of the car with a gun in his hand. Wisely, she did not unlock the door. For the next two or three minutes, which seemed like an eternity, she was a horrified spectator to an event happening at her eye level, just outside the driver's window.

The young man pushed the gun against my stomach and said, "Give me your money." I took the wallet out of my pocket and showed him it was empty. I wasn't even wearing a watch I could offer him because my watchband had broken earlier that day. I offered him some coins I had in my pocket, but he growled a rejection.

"Give me your car keys," he demanded. "They are in the car," I told him. "Tell her to open the car," he replied. For a moment I considered the new possibilities that would present, and then I refused. He was furious. He jabbed me in the stomach with his gun and said, "Do it, or I'll kill you."

Although this event happened 22 years ago, I remember it as clearly as if it were yesterday. I read somewhere that nothing concentrates the mind as wonderfully as having someone stand in front of you with a deadly weapon and tell you he intends to kill you. When I refused, the young robber repeated his demands, this time emphasizing them with an angrier tone and more motion with his gun. I remember thinking that he probably wouldn't shoot me on purpose, but if he wasn't careful in the way he kept jabbing that gun into my stomach, he might shoot me by mistake. His gun looked like a cheap one, and I was nervous about its firing mechanism.

"Give me your money." "I don't have any." "Give me your car keys." "They're in the car." "Tell her to open the car." "I won't do it." "I'll kill you if you don't." "I won't do it."

Inside the car June couldn't hear the conversation, but she could see the action with the gun. She agonized over what she should do. Should she unlock the door? Should she honk the horn? Should she drive away? Everything she considered seemed to have the possibility of making matters worse, so she just waited and prayed. Then a peaceful feeling came over her. She felt it would be all right.

Then, for the first time, I saw the possibility of help. From behind the robber, a city bus approached. It stopped about twenty feet away. A passenger stepped off and scurried away. The driver looked directly at me, but I could see that he was not going to offer any assistance.

While this was happening behind the young robber, out of his view, he became nervous and distracted. His gun wavered from my stomach until its barrel pointed slightly to my left. My arm was already partly raised, and with a quick motion I could seize the gun and struggle with him without the likelihood of being shot. I was taller and heavier than this young man, and at that time of my life was somewhat athletic. I had no doubt that I could prevail in a quick wrestling match if I could get his gun out of the contest.

Just as I was about to make my move, I had a unique experience. I did not see anything or hear anything, but I knew something. I knew what would happen if I grabbed that gun. We would struggle, and I would turn the gun into that young man's chest. It would fire, and he would die. I also understood that I must not have the blood of that young man on my conscience for the rest of my life.

I relaxed, and as the bus pulled away I followed an impulse to put my right hand on his shoulder and give him a lecture. June and I had some teenage children at that time, and giving lectures came naturally.

"Look here," I said. "This isn't right. What you're doing just isn't right. The next car might be a policeman, and you could get killed or sent to jail for this."

With the gun back in my stomach, the young robber replied to my lecture by going through his demands for the third time. But this time his voice was subdued. When he offered the final threat to kill me, he didn't sound persuasive. When I refused again, he hesitated for a moment and then stuck the gun in his pocket and ran away. June unlocked the door, and we drove off, uttering a prayer of thanks. We had experienced the kind of miraculous protection illustrated in the Bible stories I had read as a boy.

I have often pondered the significance of that event in relation to the responsibilities that came later in my life. Less than a year after that August night, I was chosen as president of Brigham Young University. Almost fourteen years after that experience, I received my present calling.

I am grateful that the Lord gave me the vision and strength to refrain from trusting in the arm of flesh and to put my trust in the protecting care of our Heavenly Father. I am grateful for the Book of Mormon promise to us of the last days that "the righteous need not fear," for the Lord "will preserve the righteous by his power" (1 Nephi 22:17). I am grateful for the protection promised to those who have kept their covenants and qualified for the blessings promised in sacred places. 🪔

"Why Have You Kept It a Secret?"

Open your mouths and spare not, and you shall be laden
with sheaves upon your backs, for lo, I am with you.
—D&C 33:9

Elder Robert C. Oaks

Consider that you are invited to a friend's house for breakfast. On the table you see a large pitcher of freshly squeezed orange juice from which your host fills his glass. But he offers you none. Finally, you ask, "Could I have a glass of orange juice?"

He replies, "Oh, I am sorry. I was afraid you might not like orange juice, and I didn't want to offend you by offering you something you didn't desire."

Now, that sounds absurd, but it is not too different from the way we hesitate to offer up something far sweeter than orange juice. I have often worried how I would answer some friend about my hesitancy when I meet him beyond the veil.

A story related by Elder Christoffel Golden, of South Africa, refreshed my concerns. He was recently in Lusaka, Zambia, attending a meeting of new converts. A well-spoken, well-dressed stranger with a Book of Mormon in hand walked in. He stated he had driven past the chapel many times and had wondered what church met there and what they taught for doctrine.

At the conclusion of the meeting, this gentleman stood up, raised his copy of the Book of Mormon high in the air, and asked, "Why have you kept this book hidden from the people of Lusaka? Why have you kept it a secret?"

As I heard this story, I flinched that one day some friend might ask me, "Why have you kept this Book of Mormon, with its message of truth and salvation, a secret?"

My reply, "I was afraid I would damage our friendship," will not be very satisfying to either me or my friend. 🐚

Worldly Promises

SISTER BONNIE L. OSCARSON

And he shall plant in the hearts of the children the promises made to the fathers, and the hearts of the children shall turn to their fathers.

Joseph Smith—History 1:39

Agnes Hoggan and her husband joined the Church in Scotland in 1861. Suffering great persecution in their homeland, they immigrated to America with their children. Several years later, Agnes became a widow with eight children to support and worked hard to keep them fed and clothed. Her 12-year-old daughter, Isabelle, was lucky enough to find employment as a servant to a wealthy, non-LDS family.

Isabelle lived in their large home and helped look after their younger children. In exchange for her services, a small wage was paid each week to her mother. Isabelle was soon accepted as a member of the family and began to enjoy many of the same privileges, such as taking dance lessons, wearing beautiful clothing, and attending the theater. This arrangement continued for four years, until the family for whom Isabelle worked was transferred to another state. They had grown so fond of Isabelle that they approached her mother, Agnes, and asked for permission to legally adopt her. They promised they would provide her with a good education, see that she married well, and make her an heir to their estate with their own children. They would also continue to make payments to Agnes.

This struggling widow and mother had a hard decision to make, but she did not hesitate for a moment. Listen to the words of her granddaughter, written many years later: "If her love had not compelled [her] to say no, she had an even better reason—she had come all the way from Scotland and had gone through tribulations and trials for the Gospel, and she did not intend, if humanly possible, to let a child of hers lose what she had come so far to gain." The wealthy family used every possible argument, and Isabelle herself cried and begged to be allowed to go, but Agnes remained firm. As you can imagine, 16-year-old Isabelle felt as if her life was ruined.

Isabelle Hoggan is my great-grandmother, and I am most grateful for the testimony and conviction that burned so brightly in her mother's heart, which did not allow her to trade her daughter's membership in the Church for worldly promises. Today, hundreds of her descendants who enjoy the blessings of membership in the Church are the beneficiaries of Agnes's deep-seated faith and conversion to the gospel. &

A Voice amid All the Noise

Thou shalt hearken to the voice of the Lord thy God,
to keep all his commandments which I command thee this day.
—Deuteronomy 13:18

Elder Allan F. Packer

When I was a young man in high school, one of my passions was American football. I played middle linebacker. The coach worked the team hard, teaching us the basics. We practiced until the skills became natural and automatic.

During one play against our biggest rival, I had an experience that has helped me over the years. We were on defense. I knew my assigned opponent, and as the play unfolded, he moved to my right into the line of scrimmage. There was a lot of noise from players and fans. I reacted as the coach had taught us and followed my man into the line, not knowing if he had the ball. To my surprise, I felt the ball partially in my hands. I gave it a tug, but my opponent didn't let go. As we tugged back and forth, amid all the noise I heard a voice yelling, "Packer, tackle him!" That was enough to bring me to my senses, so I dropped him on the spot.

I have wondered how I heard that voice above all the other noise. I had become acquainted with the voice of the coach during the practices, and I had learned to trust it. I knew that what he taught worked. We need to be acquainted with the promptings of the Holy Ghost, and we need to practice and apply gospel teachings until they become natural and automatic. These promptings become the foundation of our testimonies. Then our testimonies will keep us happy and safe in troubled times.

PRESIDENT BOYD K. PACKER

The song of the righteous is a prayer unto me,
and it shall be answered with a blessing upon their heads.
—D&C 25:12

My brother, Colonel Leon C. Packer, was stationed at the Pentagon in Washington, D.C. A much decorated B-24 pilot, he became a brigadier general in the Air Force. While I was at Langley Field, the war in Europe ended, and so we were ordered to the Pacific. I spent a few days with Leon in Washington before shipping out for combat.

He told me of things he had learned under fire. He flew from North Africa on raids over southern Europe; very few of those planes returned.

On April 16, 1943, he was captain of a B-24 bomber returning to England after a raid in Europe. His plane, the *Yard Bird,* was heavily damaged by flak and dropped out of formation.

Then they were alone and came under heavy attack from fighters.

His one-page account of that experience says: "Number three engine was smoking and the prop ran away. Number four fuel line was shot out. Right aileron cables and stabilizer cables were shot out. Rudders partially locked. Radio shot out. Extremely large holes in the right wing. Flaps shot out. Entire rear part of the fuselage filled with holes. Hydraulic system shot out. Tail turret out."

A history of the Eighth Air Force, published just two years ago, gives a detailed account of that flight written by one of the crew. With one engine on fire, the other three lost power. They were going down. The alarm bell ordered that they bail out. The bombardier, the only one able to get out, parachuted into the English Channel.

The pilots left their seats and made their way toward the bomb bay to bail out. Suddenly Leon heard an engine cough and sputter. He quickly climbed back to his seat and coaxed enough power from the engines to reach the coast of England. Then the engines failed, and they crashed.

The landing gear was shorn off on the brow of a hill; the plane plowed through trees and crumbled. Dirt filled the fuselage.

Amazingly, though some were terribly wounded, all aboard survived. The bombardier was lost, but he probably saved the lives of the other nine. When smoke poured from the engines and a parachute appeared, the fighters stopped their attack. That was not the only time Leon had crash-landed.

As we visited, he told me how he was able to hold himself together under fire. He said, "I have a favorite hymn"—and he named it—"and when things got rough I would sing it silently to myself, and there would come a faith and an assurance that kept me on course."

He sent me off to combat with that lesson.

In the spring of 1945 I was able to test that lesson Leon had taught me those months before.

The war in the Pacific ended before we reached the Philippines, and we were ordered to Japan. One day we flew out of Atsugi airfield near Yokohama in a B-17 bomber bound for Guam to pick up a beacon light.

After nine hours in the air, we let down through the clouds to find ourselves hopelessly lost. Our radio was out. We were, as it turned out, in a typhoon.

Flying just above the ocean, we began a search pattern. In that desperate situation, I remembered the words of my brother. I learned that you can pray and even sing without making a sound. After some time we pulled up over a line of rocks jutting out of the water. Could they be part of the chain of the Mariana Islands? We followed them. Soon Tinian Island loomed ahead, and we landed with literally seconds of fuel in the tank. As we headed down the runway, the engines one by one stopped. I learned that both prayer and music can be very silent and very personal.

Now, while that experience was dramatic, the greater value of Leon's lesson came later in everyday life when I faced the same temptations you young people and children face now. As the years passed I found that, while not easy, I could control my thoughts if I made a place for them to go. You can replace thoughts of temptation, anger, disappointment, or fear with better thoughts—with music.

I love the sacred music of the Church. The hymns of the Restoration carry an inspiration and a protection. 🎵

A Glass
of Milk

ELDER L. TOM PERRY

When we obtain any blessing from God, it is by obedience
to that law upon which it is predicated.
—*D&C 130:21*

remember that as a young executive many years ago, part of my job involved attending dinners sponsored by different business groups. Each dinner was always preceded by a social hour. I felt very uncomfortable in these settings. After the first one or two dinners, I started coming late to miss the social hour. My boss thought this was not a good practice because I was missing valuable time associating with business leaders. Still, I felt awkward visiting in groups where I was the only one without a drink in my hand. I kept wondering what to do with my hands. You can always put one hand in your pocket, but you look a little foolish with both of them there. I tried holding a glass of 7-Up, but it had the appearance of an alcoholic beverage.

Finally I went over to the bartender and asked him if he had any drink that was distinctively different in appearance from an alcoholic beverage. He went into the kitchen and came back with a half gallon of milk and poured me a glass. Pouring a glass of milk at a cocktail hour was a unique event. It seemed to attract the attention of everyone, and I became the target of a lot of jesting. It embarrassed me at first, until I discovered that I was meeting more business leaders than I had at any previous gathering. I found that I did not have to violate Church standards to become a viable, contributing member of

my chosen profession. It was more the case that success came because I did adhere to my values.

It soon became a practice at the social hours in that community to always have a carton of milk on the bar. I was amazed, as time passed, by how many of my associates were joining me for a glass of milk during the hour that we spent together. I found, just as Daniel did, that being different in the world brought some interesting reactions, but obedience to the Lord's law is always associated with His blessings. Isn't that the message of the revelation contained in the Doctrine and Covenants?

"There is a law, irrevocably decreed in heaven before the foundations of this world, upon which all blessings are predicated—

"And when we obtain any blessing from God, it is by obedience to that law upon which it is predicated" (D&C 130:20–21).

Wrapped in a Clean Handkerchief

SISTER ANNE C. PINGREE

Ye know how we exhorted and comforted and charged every one of you,
as a father doth his children, that ye would walk worthy of God,
who hath called you unto his kingdom and glory.
—1 Thessalonians 2:11–12

I will never forget a sauna-hot day in the lush rain forest of southeastern Nigeria. My husband and I had traveled to one of the most remote locations in our mission so he could conduct temple recommend interviews with members in the Ikot Eyo district. Some in this growing district had been Church members less than two years. All the members lived 3,000 miles away from the nearest temple in Johannesburg, South Africa. None had received their temple endowment.

These members knew the appointed day each month we would come to their district, but even we didn't know the exact hour we would arrive; nor could we call, for telephones were rare in that part of West Africa. So these committed African Saints gathered early in the morning to wait all day if necessary for their temple recommend interviews. When we arrived, I noticed among those waiting in the searing heat were two Relief Society sisters dressed in bold-patterned wrappers, white blouses, and the traditional African head-ties.

Many hours later, after all the interviews were completed, as my husband and I drove back along that sandy jungle trail, we were stunned when we saw these two sisters still walking. We realized they had trekked from their village—a distance of 18 miles round trip—just to obtain a temple recommend they knew they would never have the privilege of using.

These Nigerian Saints believed the counsel of President Howard W. Hunter: "It would please the Lord for every adult member to be worthy of—and to carry—a current temple recommend, even if proximity to a temple does not allow immediate or frequent use of it." In her hand, carefully wrapped in a clean handkerchief, each sister carried her precious temple recommend. I carry their examples of faith carefully wrapped in my heart. ◌

Elder Ronald A. Rasband

Thou hast found grace in my sight, and I know thee by name.
—Exodus 33:17

Throughout my life, I have come to know through my own experiences that Heavenly Father hears and answers our personal prayers. I know that Jesus is the living Christ and that He knows each of us individually, or as the scriptures express it, "one by one" (3 Nephi 11:15; 17:21). During the final months of our mission, we experienced an event that taught once again this profound principle that each of us is known and loved by God.

Elder Neal A. Maxwell was coming to New York City for some Church business, and we were informed that he would also like to have a mission conference. We were so pleased to have this opportunity to hear from one of the Lord's chosen servants. I was asked to select one of our missionaries to provide the opening prayer for the meeting. I might have randomly picked one of the missionaries to pray, but felt to ponder and prayerfully select one whom the Lord would have me ask. As I was going through the missionary roster, a name boldly stood out to me: Elder Joseph Appiah of Accra, Ghana. He was the one I felt the Lord wanted to pray at the meeting.

Prior to the mission conference, I was having a regularly scheduled interview with Elder Appiah and told him of the prompting that I had received for him to pray. With amazement and humility in his eyes, he began to weep deeply. Somewhat surprised by his reaction, I started to tell him that it was all right and he wouldn't have to pray, when he informed me he would love to offer the prayer, that his emotion was caused by the love he has for Elder Maxwell. He told me that this Apostle is very special to the Saints in Ghana and to his own family. Elder Maxwell had called his father to be the district president in Accra and had sealed his mother and father in the Salt Lake Temple.

Now, I didn't know any of what I just related about this missionary or his family, but the Lord did and inspired a mission president on behalf of *one* missionary to provide a lifelong memory and testimony-building experience.

At the meeting, Elder Appiah offered a wonderful prayer and made a humble contribution to a meeting where Elder Maxwell taught the missionaries of the attributes of Jesus Christ. All who were there will never forget the feelings of love they experienced for their Savior. 🔖

He Knows Us

SISTER SYDNEY S. REYNOLDS

*Bring ye all the tithes into the storehouse, that there may be meat
in mine house, and prove me now herewith, saith the Lord of hosts,
if I will not open you the windows of heaven, and pour you out
a blessing, that there shall not be room enough to receive it.*
—Malachi 3:10

$\mathcal{M}$any years ago John Orth worked in a foundry in Australia, and in a terrible accident, hot molten lead splashed onto his face and body. He was administered to, and some of the vision was restored to his right eye, but he was completely blind in his left. Because he couldn't see well, he lost his job. He tried to get employment with his wife's family, but their business failed due to the depression. He was forced to go door-to-door seeking odd jobs and handouts to pay for food and rent.

One year he did not pay any tithing and went to talk to the branch president. The branch president understood the situation but asked John to make it a matter of prayer and fasting so that he could find a way to pay his tithing. John and his wife, Alice, fasted and prayed and determined that the only thing of value they owned was her engagement ring—a beautiful ring bought in happier times. After much anguish they decided to take the ring to a pawnbroker and learned it was worth enough to pay their tithing and some other outstanding bills. That Sunday he went in to the branch president and paid his tithing. As he left the office, he happened to meet the mission president, who noticed his damaged eyes.

Brother Orth's son, now serving as a bishop in Adelaide, later wrote: "We believe that [the mission president] was an eye doctor, for he was commonly called President Dr. Rees. He spoke to Dad and was able to examine him and offer suggestions to help his eyesight. Dad followed his advice, . . . and in due course sight was restored—15 percent sight to his left eye and 95 percent sight to his right eye—and with the

help of glasses he could see again." With his vision restored, John was never unemployed again; redeemed the ring, which is now a family heirloom; and paid a full tithing for the rest of his life. The Lord knew John Orth, and He knew who could help him.

"President Dr. Rees" was my mother's father, and he probably never knew of the miracle that was wrought that day. Generations were blessed because a family decided they would pay their tithing regardless of the difficulty—and then met a man who "happened by" and "happened" to be an eye surgeon who was able to make a great difference in their life. While some may be tempted to believe these are just coincidences, I have confidence that even a sparrow cannot fall to the ground but He knows it. &

The Still, Small Voice

PRESIDENT MARION G. ROMNEY

If ye will enter in by the way, and receive the Holy Ghost,
it will show unto you all things what ye should do.
—2 Nephi 32:5

I was once concluding a talk I had given at the funeral of a fine Latter-day Saint mother and was almost ready to say amen and sit down. There came into my mind the words, "Turn around and bear your testimony." And this I did. I thought no more about the event for several months until my sister, then living in a neighboring stake, paid us a visit and told us this incident:

She said: "There lives in our ward a woman who for many years has taken no interest in the Church. Our efforts to activate her have been fruitless. Recently she has completely changed. She pays her tithing, attends sacrament meetings regularly, and participates in all Church activities. When asked what caused the reformation, she said: 'I went to Salt Lake City to the funeral of my mother. During the services a man by the name of Romney spoke. After he had given an ordinary talk, I thought he was going to sit down; but instead he turned around to the pulpit and bore a testimony which greatly impressed me. It awakened in me a desire to live as my mother had always taught me.'"

Now I know, my brothers and sisters and friends, and bear witness to the fact that revelation from the Lord comes through the spoken word, by personal visitation, by messengers from the Lord, through dreams, and by way of visions, and by the voice of the Lord coming into one's mind.

Most often, however, revelation comes to us by means of the still, small voice.

ELDER R. CONRAD SHULTZ

Remember the awfulness in transgressing against that Holy God, and also
the awfulness of yielding to the enticings of that cunning one. Remember,
to be carnally-minded is death, and to be spiritually-minded is life eternal.
—2 Nephi 9:39

*I*n this world in which we live, things are not always what they appear to be.
We sometimes are unaware of the powerful forces pulling on us. Appearances
can be very deceptive.

A few years ago I had an experience with deceptive appearances where the results
could have been tragic. My wife's cousin and family were visiting us from Utah. It was a
calm summer day on the Oregon coast, and we were fishing in the ocean. It was pleasant, and we were having a good time catching salmon, when for some reason I turned
around to see a huge eight-foot wave bearing down upon us. I only had time to shout a
warning before the wave hit us broadside. Somehow the boat stayed upright, but Gary,
our cousin, was thrown overboard. We were all wearing life jackets and with some difficulty maneuvered the boat, half filled with water, to where he was floating and pulled
him aboard.

We had been hit by what is called a sneaker wave. It doesn't happen often, and
there is no way to predict an occurrence. Later we found that up and down the Oregon-
Washington coast, five people had drowned that day in three separate boating accidents.
All were caused by the same sneaker wave, which for no apparent reason had welled up

off the ocean surface. At the time we went out over the bar, the ocean was flat and calm and gave no sign of any danger. But the ocean turned out to be very deceptive and not at all what it appeared to be.

As we make our way through this life's journey, we must continually be on guard and watch for those things which are deceptive and not what they appear to be. If we are not careful, the sneaker waves in life can be as deadly as those in the ocean. . . .

I am grateful that we had on our life jackets that summer day on the ocean. I am thankful we were able to avoid the tragedy that came to others from that sneaker wave. It is my prayer that we will continue to wear our life jackets of obedience in order to avoid the tragedy that will surely come if we are deceived and follow the enticings of the adversary. 🐚

Simple Messages of Love

ELDER RICHARD G. SCOTT

*Husbands, love your wives, even as Christ also
loved the church, and gave himself for it.*
—*Ephesians 5:25*

I learned from my wife the importance of expressions of love. Early in our marriage, often I would open my scriptures to give a message in a meeting, and I would find an affectionate, supportive note Jeanene had slipped into the pages. Sometimes they were so tender that I could hardly talk. Those preciousnotes from a loving wife were and continue to be a priceless treasure of comfort and inspiration.

I began to do the same thing with her, not realizing how much it truly meant to her. I remember one year we didn't have the resources for me to give her a valentine, so I decided to paint a watercolor on the front of the refrigerator. I did the best I could; only I made one mistake. It was enamel paint, not watercolor. She never let me try to remove that permanent paint from the refrigerator.

I remember one day I took some of those little round paper circles that form when you punch holes in paper, and I wrote on them the numbers 1 to 100. I turned each over and wrote her a message, one word on each circle. Then I scooped them up and put them in an envelope. I thought she would get a good laugh.

When she passed away, I found in her private things how much she appreciated the simple messages that we shared with each other. I noted that she had carefully pasted every one of those circles on a piece of paper. She not only kept my notes to her, but she protected them with plastic coverings as if they were a valuable treasure. There is only one that she didn't put with the others. It is still behind the glass in our kitchen clock. It reads, "Jeanene, it is time to tell you I love you." It remains there and reminds me of that exceptional daughter of Father in Heaven.

As I have thought back over our life together, I realize how blessed we've been. We have not had arguments in our home or unkind words between us. Now I realize that blessing came because of her. It resulted from her willingness to give, to share, and to never think of herself. &

The Greater Wealth

Elder Steven E. Snow

All things denote there is a God; yea, even the earth,
and all things that are upon the face of it.
—Alma 30:44

Growing up in southern Utah, some of us sought employment at the many gasoline service stations that lined old Highway 91 as it made its way through downtown St. George. My younger brother, Paul, then 18, worked at Tom's Service, a station located about three blocks from our home.

One summer day, a car with New York license plates pulled in the station and asked for a fill-up. (In those days someone actually came out and filled your car with gas, washed your windows, and checked your oil.) While Paul was washing the windshield, the driver asked him how far it was to the Grand Canyon.

Paul replied that it was 170 miles.

"I've waited all my life to see the Grand Canyon," the man exclaimed. "What's it like out there?"

"I don't know," Paul answered, "I've never been there."

"You mean to tell me," the man responded, "that you live two and a half hours from one of the seven wonders of the world and you've never been there!"

"That's right," Paul said.

After a moment, the man replied, "Well, I guess I can understand that. My wife and I have lived in Manhattan for over 20 years, and we've never visited the Statue of Liberty."

"I've been there," Paul said.

Isn't it ironic that we will often travel many miles to see the wonders of nature or the creations of man, but yet ignore the beauty in our own backyard?

It is human nature, I suppose, to seek elsewhere for our happiness. Pursuit of career goals, wealth, and material rewards can cloud our perspective and often leads to a lack of appreciation for the bounteous blessings of our present circumstances. It is precarious to dwell on why we have not been given more. It is, however, beneficial and humbling to dwell on why we have been given so much.

An old proverb states, "The greater wealth is contentment with a little." 🐚

Lift Where You Stand

PRESIDENT DIETER F. UCHTDORF

And the Lord called his people Zion, because they were of one heart and one mind, and dwelt in righteousness.

—Moses 7:18

Some years ago in our meetinghouse in Darmstadt, Germany, a group of brethren was asked to move a grand piano from the chapel to the adjoining cultural hall, where it was needed for a musical event. None were professional movers, and the task of getting that gravity-friendly instrument through the chapel and into the cultural hall seemed nearly impossible. Everybody knew that this task required not only physical strength but also careful coordination. There were plenty of ideas, but not one could keep the piano balanced correctly. They repositioned the brethren by strength, height, and age over and over again—nothing worked.

As they stood around the piano, uncertain of what to do next, a good friend of mine, Brother Hanno Luschin, spoke up. He said, "Brethren, stand close together and lift where you stand."

It seemed too simple. Nevertheless, each lifted where he stood, and the piano rose from the ground and moved into the cultural hall as if on its own power. That was the answer to the challenge. They merely needed to stand close together and lift where they stood. . . .

Brethren, as strong as you are, you cannot and you should not lift a piano by yourself. Likewise, none of us can or should move the Lord's work alone. But if we all stand close together in the place the Lord has appointed and lift where we stand, nothing can keep this divine work from moving upward and forward.

May we always remember this profound lesson: that we are banner bearers of the Lord Jesus Christ, upheld by the Holy Spirit of God, faithful and true to the end, each one devoted to give our all to the cause of Zion and bound by covenant to stand close together and lift where we stand. 🔥

"The Only Person I Baptized"

ELDER W. CHRISTOPHER WADDELL

*Are not two sparrows sold for a farthing? and one of them shall not fall on the
ground without your Father. But the very hairs of your head are all numbered.
Fear ye not therefore, ye are of more value than many sparrows.*

—Matthew 10:29–31

A few years ago, Elder Javier Misiego, from Madrid, Spain, was serving a full-time mission in Arizona. At that time, his mission call to the United States appeared somewhat unusual, as most young men from Spain were being called to serve in their own country.

At the conclusion of a stake fireside, where he and his companion had been invited to participate, Elder Misiego was approached by a less-active member of the Church who had been brought by a friend. It was the first time this man had been inside a chapel in years. Elder Misiego was asked if he might know a José Misiego in Madrid. When Elder Misiego responded that his father's name was José Misiego, the man excitedly asked a few more questions to confirm that this was *the* José Misiego. When it was determined that they were speaking about the same man, this less-active member began to weep. "Your father was the only person I baptized during my entire mission," he explained and described how his mission had been, in his mind, a failure. He attributed his years of inactivity to some feelings of inadequacy and concern, believing that he had somehow let the Lord down.

Elder Misiego then described what this supposed failure of a missionary meant to his family. He told him that his father, baptized as a young single adult, had married in the temple, that Elder Misiego was the fourth of six children, that all three boys and a sister had served full-time missions, that all were active in the Church, and that all who were married had been sealed in the temple.

The less-active returned missionary began to sob. Through his efforts, he now learned, scores of lives had been blessed, and the Lord had sent an elder from Madrid, Spain, all the way to a fireside in Arizona to let him know that he had not been a failure. The Lord knows where He wants each missionary to serve.

Even as a Child

ELDER ROBERT J. WHETTEN

For the natural man is an enemy to God, . . . and will be, forever and ever,
unless he yields to the enticings of the Holy Spirit, . . . and becometh as a
child, submissive, meek, humble, patient, full of love.
—Mosiah 3:19

One January an earthquake in the central mountain region of Colombia left the city of Armenia devastated. Concerned stake presidents called the Area Presidency in Quito to find out what the needs of the members living in Armenia were. The district president confirmed that many Church members had lost their homes and had found shelter in the four undamaged chapels but urgently needed food and clothing. The Relief Society and priesthood leaders swung into action, and donations from members throughout Colombia poured into a designated chapel in each city. Seven-year-old Neidi had come with her parents to the chapel in the city of Cali and watched as Bishop Villareal received donations from members.

"Bishop, how can I help the children in Armenia?"

"Neidi, your parents have already helped."

She went to the other end of the chapel and observed that little clothing and no shoes for children were being packed. Neidi came back to the bishop with her shoes in her hand. "Now I know how I can help. Please give these shoes to another little girl in Armenia who has lost hers." Her bare feet made no sound as she slipped away. 🔔

Elder Joseph B. Wirthlin

Stand ye in holy places, and be not moved, until the day of
the Lord come; for behold, it cometh quickly, saith the Lord.
—*D&C 87:8*

On December 26, 2004, a powerful earthquake struck off the coast of Indonesia, creating a deadly tsunami that killed more than 200,000 people. It was a terrible tragedy. In one day, millions of lives were forever changed.

But there was one group of people who, although their village was destroyed, did not suffer a single casualty.

The reason?

They knew a tsunami was coming.

The Moken people live in villages on islands off the coast of Thailand and Burma (Myanmar). A society of fishermen, their lives depend on the sea. For hundreds and perhaps thousands of years, their ancestors have studied the ocean, and they have passed their knowledge down from father to son.

One thing in particular they were careful to teach was what to do when the ocean receded. According to their traditions, when that happened, the "Laboon"—a wave that eats people—would arrive soon after.

When the elders of the village saw the dreaded signs, they shouted to everyone to run to high ground.

Not everyone listened.

One elderly fisherman said, "None of the kids believed me." In fact, his own daughter called him a liar. But the old fisherman would not relent until all had left the village and climbed to higher ground.

The Moken people were fortunate in that they had someone with conviction who warned them of what would follow. The villagers were fortunate because they listened. Had they not, they may have perished.

The prophet Nephi wrote about the great disaster of his day, the destruction of Jerusalem. "As one generation hath been destroyed among the Jews because of iniquity," he said, "even so have they been destroyed from generation to generation according to their iniquities; and never hath any of them been destroyed save it were foretold them by the prophets of the Lord" (2 Nephi 25:9).

Since the days of Adam, the Lord has spoken to His prophets, and while His message differs according to the specific needs of the time, there is one consistent, never-changing theme: Depart from iniquity and journey to higher ground. 🐚

The Boy Who Prayed with Perfect Trust

SISTER DWAN J. YOUNG

Ask, and ye shall receive; knock, and it shall be opened unto you;
for he that asketh, receiveth; and unto him that knocketh, it shall be opened.

—*3 Nephi 27:29*

Part of seeking is to give space for an answer. After you have asked for help, pause and listen. Many times the Lord answers our prayers in a still, small voice. It may be an answer you don't want to hear. Or you may not recognize what happens to you as an answer to your prayers.

I'll give you an example. Three little boys were flying a kite in a field away from their homes. It began to rain, and they wanted to save their kite. As they hastily pulled it from the sky, it caught on a tree limb high over their heads.

They found a long stick and tried to pull it down, but they couldn't reach it. They tried everything they could think of to get it down, but the kite just turned and twisted in the storm. One of the boys finally said to the others, "I think we should pray." The other two looked at him, then followed his lead, bowing their heads while he said the words. As they opened their eyes, they saw a car coming toward them down the road that led to the field. As it neared, the boys stood motionless and almost breathless, staring at the lady driving the car.

Their stares fascinated the lady, so she stopped and called to them, "Are you having trouble?"

"Yes," they said. "Our kite is caught on the tree. Will you help us get it down?"

"I'll try," she said. "Stand away while I back up."

She backed her car to position it under the kite, then she got out, climbed on top of the car, and with the long stick retrieved the kite.

When the boy who had offered the prayer carried his kite into the kitchen, he told his mother about the kite's getting caught in the tree. She asked, "Who helped you get your kite down?"

"Heavenly Father," he replied. The boy, who had prayed with perfect trust, knew the answer to a prayer when he saw it. ⚜

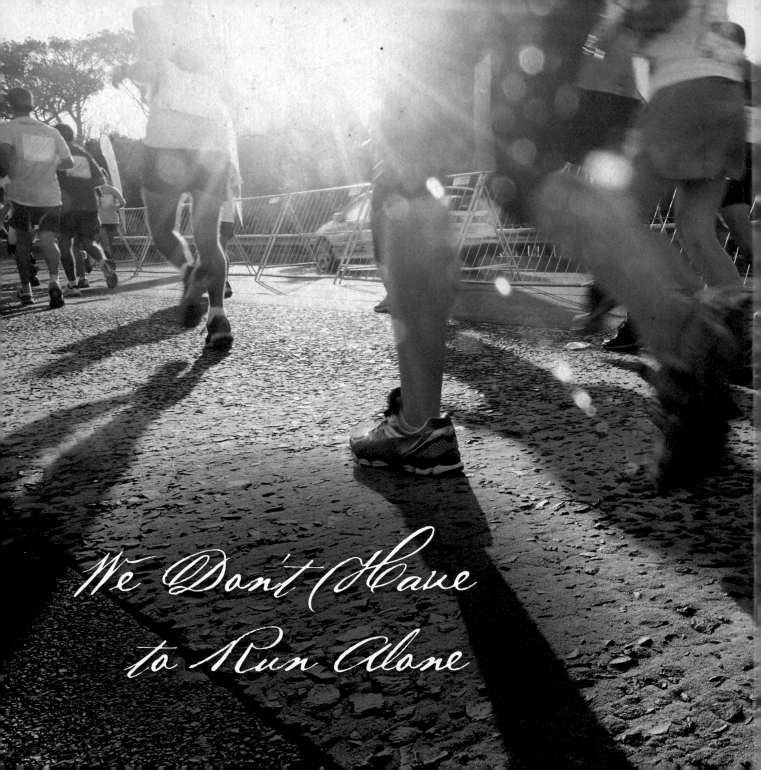

We Don't Have
to Run Alone

Elder W. Craig Zwick

*Let us lay aside every weight, and the sin
which doth so easily beset us, and let us run
with patience the race that is set before us.*
—Hebrews 12:1

We can never complete "the race that is set before us" (Hebrews 12:1) without placing our hand in the Lord's. Several years ago, our only daughter decided to compete in a marathon. She trained and worked very hard, along with some of her friends. The race was difficult, and there were times when she wanted to quit. But she kept going, just concentrating on one step at a time. As she was approaching the middle part of the course, she heard someone behind her shout out, "Blind man on your left."

She turned her head only to see a blind man overtake her, holding the hand of another man. They were both running the race. As they passed, she could see how tightly the blind man held the hand of his friend.

Overcome with her own physical pain, she was

lifted as she watched these two men run hand in hand. He who could see was motivated by his blind friend, and the blind man depended upon the connection he had to his friend's hand. Our daughter knew the blind man could never finish the race alone. She was inspired by the trust of the blind man and the devoted love of his friend.

In like manner, the Savior has stretched forth His hand to each of us so that we don't have to run alone. As we advance toward the finish line, He will be there to save us; and for all this He gave His life.

Photo Credits